Thomas Gisborne

The Principles of Moral Philosophy investigated

And briefly applied to the Constitution of Civil Society

Thomas Gisborne

The Principles of Moral Philosophy investigated
And briefly applied to the Constitution of Civil Society

ISBN/EAN: 9783337069537

Printed in Europe, USA, Canada, Australia, Japan

Cover: Foto ©ninafisch / pixelio.de

More available books at **www.hansebooks.com**

THE
PRINCIPLES
OF
MORAL PHILOSOPHY

INVESTIGATED,

AND BRIEFLY APPLIED TO THE CONSTITUTION
OF CIVIL SOCIETY:

TOGETHER WITH

REMARKS

ON

THE PRINCIPLE ASSUMED BY MR. PALEY AS THE BASIS OF
ALL MORAL CONCLUSIONS,

AND ON OTHER POSITIONS OF THE SAME AUTHOR.

By THOMAS GISBORNE, M. A.

LONDON:
PRINTED BY T. BENSLEY,
FOR B. WHITE AND SON, HORACE'S HEAD, FLEET-STREET.
M,DCC,LXXXIX.

TO THE

MEMBERS

OF THE

UNIVERSITY OF CAMBRIDGE,

THE

FOLLOWING TREATISE

IS RESPECTFULLY DEDICATED.

PREFACE.

THE subsequent Treatise was occasioned by an appointment, which I understand to have taken place in the University of Cambridge, that candidates for the degree of Bachelor of Arts shall be examined in the "Elements of "Moral and Political Philosophy."

No one can rejoice more sincerely than myself at every academical regulation, which facilitates the study of morality; a study of universal importance, and deserving of the utmost encouragement in a seminary particularly designed to complete the education of Christian ministers. Nor can any one be more fully convinced of the purity of the motives which gave rise to the appointment which I have mentioned, or more willing to bear ample testimony to the excellence of various parts of Mr. Paley's work. Yet I am also persuaded that the principle assumed by

Mr. Paley, as the criterion of moral duty, is open to fundamental objections of the utmost magnitude; and that many of his conclusions are not such as just reasoning would establish. As I shall hereafter state the general causes likely to facilitate the reception of any erroneous opinions maintained in the work in question, I shall at present only observe, that those opinions must operate with particular force, when apparently sanctioned by the approbation of the University; and with consequences particularly to be lamented, when instilled into persons of that age, in which the mind is easily impressed, and liable to acquire a lasting partiality for the principles which it imbibes.

It is not my intention to hold up to public notice every error into which I may imagine Mr. Paley to have fallen, nor to construct a complete system of morality. The former would be a purpose too uncandid, the latter too presumptuous. After preparing my way by by an examination of Mr. Paley's fundamental pofition, I fhall endeavour to eftablifh principles lefs exceptionable; and fhall briefly apply them to the conftitution of civil fociety. I fhall alfo occafionally remark on fuch of Mr. Paley's conclufions as fall within my immediate plan, when they appear to me to be inaccurate, and to regard topics of fuch importance as to merit further inquiry. I am willing to believe that, in profecuting this inquiry, I fhall not forget what is due to the very refpectable author who is the fubject of it; and to hope that the fame confiderations, which have led me to inveftigate the errors of others, will teach me to acknowledge with gratitude the detection of my own.

In prefixing my name to this publication, I cannot furely be fufpected of entertaining a thought fo prepofterous, as that of inviting, in any refpect whatever, a perfonal comparifon of Mr. Paley and myfelf. The fact is, that a confiderable portion of the following pages

pages was written before I had the most distant idea of avowing them. Reflection, however, and the opinion of others, convinced me that it would be in vain to expect a short and anonymous performance to attract such a share of public attention, as to have a chance of counteracting in any degree the acknowledged sentiments of Mr. Paley; and that, by pursuing my original plan, I should at once ensure to this Treatise that total neglect and oblivion, to which a book authenticated by the signature of any individual is not usually consigned, until a fair trial has been granted, and the sentence has been found to be deserved.

I cannot close this Preface without performing an act of justice, and expressing how materially I have been indebted in many of the subsequent discussions to the important observations suggested by my excellent friend, Mr. Babington, of Rothley Temple.

Yoxall Lodge,
March 27, 1789.

CONTENTS.

PART I.

EXAMINATION OF MR. PALEY'S FUNDAMENTAL PRINCIPLE OF MORALITY.

CHAP. I. *Introductory Remarks on the "Elements of Moral and Political Philosophy."* p. 1

Chap. II. *Statement and Application of the Principle of general Expediency, according to Mr. Paley.* p. 9

Chap. III. *Presumptions against the Truth of Mr. Paley's Principle from its probable Effects on human Happiness.* p. 15

Chap. IV. *Arguments against the Truth of Mr. Paley's Principle, deduced from a Comparison*

parison of that Principle with the Scriptures. p. 23

Chap. V. *Demonstrative Refutation of Mr. Paley's Principle.* p. 29

PART II.

GENERAL RIGHTS AND OBLIGATIONS OF MEN DEDUCED FROM REASON AND REVELATION.

Chap. I. *Preliminary Remarks on the Grounds from which the Principles of human Conduct are to be derived by natural Reason—Statement of certain Principles.* p. 42

Chap. II. *The first and second Propositions demonstrated.* p. 50

Ch. III. *The third Proposition demonstrated* p. 57

Chap. IV. *The fourth Proposition demonstrated* p. 73

Chap. V.

Chap. V. *The preceding Propositions shewn to be confirmed by the Scriptures.* p. 81
Chap. VI. *On Indemnification.* p. 86
Chap. VII. *On Punishment.* p. 91
Chap. VIII. *On Slavery.* p. 95
Chap. IX. *On Property.* p. 99
Chap. X. *On Engagements.* p. 109
Chap. XI. *General Review of the natural Rights and Obligations of Men.* p. 130

PART III.

APPLICATION OF THE PRINCIPLES WHICH HAVE BEEN ESTABLISHED TO THE CONSTITUTION OF CIVIL SOCIETY.

Chap. I. *The true Ground of civil Obedience explained—Erroneous Notions refuted.* p. 136
Chap. II. *Origin of civil Government.* p. 144

Chap. II.

Chap. III. *Examination of some of Mr. Paley's Objections to the Establishment of civil Obedience on Consent.* p. 147

Chap. IV. *Mr. Paley's remaining Objections considered—Comparative View of the two Systems.* p. 162

E R R A T A.

Page 10 line 8 } *for* develope *read* develop.
54 20
25 15 *for* unlimitted *read* unlimited.
30 12 *for* tract *read* track.
34 21 *after* good *dele* the comma.
52 8 *for* the second their *read* his.

PART

PART I.

EXAMINATION OF MR. PALEY'S FUNDAMENTAL PRINCIPLE OF MORALITY.

CHAP. I.

INTRODUCTORY REMARKS ON THE "ELEMENTS OF "MORAL AND POLITICAL PHILOSOPHY."

He who offers his opinions to the world ought to be impelled by such motives as will vindicate him, to the satisfaction of candid minds, from the charge of presumption. I have already noticed, in my preface, the general grounds on which I venture to solicit attention to my sentiments on subjects of morality. Those grounds it may now be proper more fully to explain.

Mr. Paley has obtained, and has in many respects deserved, a peculiar share of public favour. The selection of the most important topics

topics for the exercife of his abilities; the fedulous induftry with which he has profecuted his refearches; the fpirit of benevolence and piety which pervades and animates his writings; thefe are merits which entitle him to the diftinguifhed regard of every friend of natural and revealed religion. Where fhall we difcover founder or more pointed arguments than thofe by which many of his pofitions are enforced? Where fhall we look for models of elucidation more appofite than the examples by which thofe arguments are illuftrated? Where is the work, in which the intricacies of abftrufe fpeculation are more conftantly accommodated to practical utility; and moral conclufions more happily applied to the incidents of common life? Yet if, into a work recommended by fo many and fo powerful confiderations, fundamental errors have been admitted; if momentous conclufions reft on principles either falfe in themfelves, or improperly applied, or infufficient to fupport all the inferences deduced from them; the probable effects on the moral conduct of men cannot fail to be in a high degree extenfive and dangerous. Every circumftance which, on the perufal of one chapter, fpreads a glow a glow of approbation over the mind of the reader, contributes to prevent him from fufpecting or difcovering the miftakes in the next. Embracing, partly from the conviction of his reafon, partly from his preconceived opinions of right and wrong, the conclufions prefented to him, he no longer doubts, if he had doubted before, the truth of the propofitions from which they are derived. Reflecting on the purity of the ftream, he forgets to examine the falubrity of the fountain from which it fprings, and of the channels through which it is conveyed.

The ftyle and arrangement adopted by former moralifts, far from captivating the attention of the ftudent, have too often taught him to confider moral inveftigations as unalluring and diftafteful. He found himfelf perplexed with intricate details, purfued through innumerable fubdivifions, and frequently difgufted with the uninterefting conclufion obtained by fo laborious a procefs. In compliance with the prejudices, the indolence, and in many refpects with the reafonable expectations, of mankind, later writers have deviated from the track of their predeceffors;

they have abandoned dry and unprofitable speculations; they have mitigated the rigour of scientific method by the elegance of flowing language; and enlivened the barrenness of strict demonstration by the graces of modest ornament. The intention was dictated by wisdom, and has been executed with ability. The labours of Mr. Paley, and of others, who have been induced by motives equally wise to adopt a similar plan, have obtained the applause, and have influenced the conduct, of numbers, who turned from former treatises on the same subjects with contempt and aversion.

While I contemplate with pleasure this more general diffusion of knowledge of the most important kind, may I not be permitted to remark that some of the causes, which have ensured to Mr. Paley's work such extensive popularity, would naturally lead the world to overlook the defects inherent in any principle, assumed by him as the ground-work of moral and political philosophy? And may I not add, that the principle which he has adopted is peculiarly calculated to captivate the generality of readers; while at the same time

many

many of his *observations and conclusions are such as tend to quiet the alarms of the rigid moralist?

The doctrine of general expediency, which constitutes utility the sole measure of the rectitude or depravity of every action, and at the same time leaves the discretion of the agent to judge of that utility, will cheerfully be embraced by those whose indolence desires a rule of conduct easy to be retained, and of universal application; by those whose vague opinions and ill-governed passions are averse to absolute and immutable restraints; and by those whose mistaken liberality of sentiment suggests that a moral agent should in every case be permitted to determine for himself, unfettered by any dictates of revelation, what actions will promote on the whole his happiness or misery. Other causes, unconnected with these prejudices and errors, will concur in producing the same effect. The seeming piety of the idea, that the rule to which the conduct of the Almighty is conformable should be the standard of human actions, will

* See Mr. Paley's remarks on general rules, and on perfect rights.

dazzle well-disposed minds. Persons of an opposite description, who may find it convenient to affect a sense of virtue which they have not, will gladly profess a principle which leaves them to the sole guidance of their own discretion.

Such is the alluring nature of Mr. Paley's general rule; and many of the inferences derived from it will accord with the reader's preconceived notions of morality. In the chapters to which I have already referred (not to particularize others) he is presented with conclusions bearing evident marks of truth and justice; and if he does not pause to consider how far they are consistent with the principle from which they are said to flow, and how far they are compatible with other parts of Mr. Paley's work, he will be persuaded that the duties which he has been used to regard as of absolute obligation continue no less indispensable under the rule of general expediency.

I apprehend, however, that the principle of expediency, employed by Mr. Paley as the basis of all his moral reasoning, is liable, in the

the hands of man, to continual mifapplication; that, in many cafes, it leads to conclufions unfavourable to human happinefs; that it is incompatible with the precepts of fcripture; and that it never was defigned, nor can poffibly be adopted, for the regulation of human conduct. In the following pages I fhall endeavour to eftablifh the validity of thefe affertions; and, in the place of general expediency, to fubftitute and apply other principles, founded on reafon, confirmed by revelation, and confequently not expofed to fimilar objections.

They, who are deeply convinced of the pernicious and indefinite effects of error, who are alarmed at the train of evils which would enfue if men were actuated, in concerns of the higheft moment, by a principle deftitute of foundation, will not deem it uninterefting to examine the validity of a doctrine, likely from its own nature, to be fo generally embraced; and, from the mode of applying it, to be fo little queftioned. I am aware of the difadvantageous terms on which a writer, unknown to the public, combats authority fo weighty as that of Mr. Paley. Yet,

whatever be the deference paid to names by the generality of mankind, an inquiry into subjects of the utmost importance we may hope, in this age and country, will be received with candid attention, not only without the concurrence of adventitious aid, but even in opposition to it. It cannot, at least, be apprehended that in our universities, consecrated to the investigation of truth, a prejudice, universally giving way, should fix its latest residence. " We [b] appear astonished when we
" see the multitude led away by sounds; but
" we should remember that, if sounds work
" miracles, it is always upon ignorance. The
" influence of names is in exact proportion to
" the want of knowledge."

[b] See Mr. Paley's preface.

CHAP.

CHAP. II.

STATEMENT AND APPLICATION OF THE PRINCIPLE OF GENERAL EXPEDIENCY ACCORDING TO MR. PALEY.

It will be proper to lay before the reader a brief ſtatement of Mr. Paley's fundamental propoſitions before I enter into an examination of their truth; and I ſhall leave them to make their full impreſſion on his mind, reſerving my objections to be unfolded in ſubſequent chapters.

After having ſhewn that thoſe rules of life by which men are ordinarily governed—the law of honour, the law of the land, and the ſcriptures—do not ſuperſede the ſtudy of ethics; the firſt being founded on caprice, ſometimes abſurd and frequently vicious; the ſecond profeſſedly omitting many duties and tolerating many crimes; and the third not containing a ſpecific determination of particular caſes which continually occur; he directs his inquiries to the conſideration of the moral ſenſe.

sense. And, having [a] proved that its existence is problematical; that its dictates, admitting its existence, cannot now be distinguished from prejudices and habits, and can derive substantial weight only from resorting to ulterior sanctions; he asserts that resort may be had to these sanctions by a surer rule, and proceeds to develope the nature and the source of moral obligation. He states that [b] all obligation consists in being urged by a violent motive resulting from the command of another; and that moral obligation [c] implies the being impelled to perform certain actions, and to abstain from others, by the expectation of future rewards and punishments, resulting from the injunctions of God. Hence he infers, that to [d] inquire what is our duty, or what we are obliged to do, in any instance,

---

[a] Though I have concurred in the general conclusions established in Mr. Paley's chapter on the moral sense, I must not be understood to acquiesce in every thing which that chapter contains. The observation that " perhaps no " maxims in morality can be assigned which are universally " true, and do not bend to circumstances," will be the subject of future disquisition.

[b] Page 57, Vol. I. Ed. 6th. 8vo. To this edition all subsequent references are made.

[c] Page 59, Vol. I.   [d] Page 62, Vol. I.

is,

is, in effect, to inquire what is the will of God in that instance.

The truth of the Christian religion having been pre-supposed, Mr. Paley observes that there are two methods of discovering the will of God on any point.

Firſt, By his expreſs declarations, when they are to be obtained, in the ſcriptures.

Secondly, By what we can diſcover of his deſigns and diſpoſition from his works; or, as we uſually call it, from the light of nature.

On the preſumption of the divine benevolence—a preſumption which Mr. Paley afterwards confirms from a conſideration of the conſtitution of nature, and which might have been ſhewn to be a fundamental principle of Chriſtianity—he concludes that * the method of aſcertaining the will of God concerning any action, by the light of nature, is to inquire

* Page 70, Vol. I.

into

into the tendency of the action to promote or diminish the general happiness.

Whatever [f] is expedient he affirms to be right. But, in consequence of having shewn [g] the necessity of all moral government being administered according to general rules, he subjoins, "It [h] must be expedient, upon the "whole, at the long run; in all its effects "collateral and remote, as well as in those "which are immediate and direct; as it is "obvious that, in computing consequences, "it makes no difference in what way, or at "what distance, they ensue."

Mr. Paley, having once established to his satisfaction the principle of general expediency, in the manner which I have stated, applies it as the sole standard not of those moral duties only concerning which the scriptures do not furnish him with sufficient information, but of all moral duties universally, of whatever nature, and however ascertained. "The "criterion [i] of right is utility." "What-

[f] Page 70, Vol. I.
[h] Page 78, Vol. I.
[g] Page 74, Vol. I.
[i] Page 71, Vol. I.

"*ever* [k] is expedient is right." "It is the *utility* of *any* moral rule *alone* which constitutes the obligation of it." He further declares that every moral rule is liable to be superseded in particular cases on the ground of expediency. "Moral philosophy [l] cannot pronounce that any rule of morality is so rigid as to bend to no exceptions; nor, on the other hand, can she comprise these exceptions within any previous description. She confesses that the obligation of every law depends upon its ultimate utility; that, this utility having a finite and determinate value, situations may be feigned, and consequently may possibly arise, in which the general tendency is outweighed by the enormity of the particular mischief;" and of course when ultimate utility, and consequently the will of God, render it as much an act of duty to break the rule, as it is on other occasions to observe it.

But who shall judge of the expediency? "Every [m] man," he replies, "for himself."

[k] P. 70, Vol. I.   [l] P. 411, Vol. II.
[m] P. 142, Vol. II.

"The[a] danger of error and abuse is no objection to the rule of expediency, because every other rule is liable to the same or greater; and every rule that can be propounded on the subject (like all rules which appeal to and bind the conscience) must in the application depend upon private judgment."

This paragraph, in which the argument is couched in general terms, equally applicable to every case of expediency, contains the language and determination of Mr. Paley on the duty of civil submission or resistance: and it contains what must be his language and determination respecting every other moral duty, as he founds all on the same principle.

[a] P. 143, Vol. II.

CHAP. III.

PRESUMPTIONS AGAINST THE TRUTH OF MR. PALEY'S PRINCIPLE FROM IT'S PROBABLE EFFECTS ON HUMAN HAPPINESS.

The refult of the ftatement contained in the preceding chapter appears to be, that, according to Mr. Paley's principle, a man is bound to the obfervance of each moral rule as long as he thinks fuch obfervance generally expedient; that he is permitted and obliged to difregard it, whenever in his opinion the violation of it will be attended upon the whole with beneficial confequences; and that with refpect to *every* moral rule fuch cafes may exift.

Before we enter into an examination of the truth or fallacy of the arguments by which this doctrine is fupported, it may be of ufe to confider its nature and tendency, and to beftow a minute attention on the effects which it would be likely to produce, if univerfally admitted

admitted, on the conduct and happiness of mankind.

A moralist, possessed, like Mr. Paley, of a sound and penetrating understanding, actuated by a sincere reverence for the scriptures, a firm attachment to virtue, and a decided abhorrence of vice; if he also concur in Mr. Paley's principle, must maintain that in certain possible cases he should deserve not merely pardon, but approbation, from his fellow-creatures, for actions which are usually deemed the blackest crimes. He must maintain that circumstances may arise which shall entitle him to the reward of everlasting glory, at the judgment-seat of Christ, for his rapine, for his hypocrisy, for his perjuries, for his murders, for having betrayed his country, or abjured his God! He must maintain that his private opinion of future consequences is the standard which alone establishes the meaning of the plainest precepts, and the obligation of the most positive injunctions, of the gospel!

From Mr. Paley's concessions it must be allowed that no one of the cases described is too extravagant to be verified by facts, or to

be

be authorised by general expediency. But if his previous declarations would have permitted him to assert that no crime, such as those which I have specified, can ever be generally expedient, (an assertion which on grounds very different from Mr. Paley's may be firmly established), his principles would still remain open to the same objection: for they would equally justify a man in the commission of any one or all of these enormities, provided he were *persuaded* of the general utility of his conduct, whether that persuasion were the result of reason, of prejudice, or of fanaticism.

Such would be the fruits of this doctrine when applied by a wise and virtuous moralist. What then would be its effects when applied by a man possessed of wisdom, but destitute of virtue? or of virtue, but destitute of wisdom? or equally deficient in both? Would it not be made to assume every form under the hand of artifice, and to countenance every practice under the control of passion and interest? How would it be narrowed and contracted, when submitted to the ignorance of the bulk of mankind, so little qualified

qualified to difcover and appreciate the various caufes of ultimate utility, to trace remote contingencies, and contemplate the defigns of Providence with a comprehenfive eye! When we are eftimating the confequences which would accrue to human happinefs from the general reception of Mr. Paley's principle, we muft take into the account not only thofe conclufions which are fairly deducible from it, but thofe alfo which we may reafonably fuppofe will be inferred, or reprefented as inferred, from it, by a confiderable part of mankind. We are further to pay particular attention to the ufe likely to be made of this doctrine by princes and men in power, as their influence over the happinefs of others is fo extenfive and fo great.

Let us confider, then, whether the admiffion of this rule would not be extremely favourable to defpotifm. A monarch is told that there is no fuch thing as right in oppofition to general expediency; and he is alfo told that *he* is to judge of that expediency. He can fcarcely meet with a principle more likely to miflead himfelf; nor need he wifh for one more convenient, when he is defirous

of

of impofing upon others. If he be a good man, confcious of the purity of his views, and ftrongly impreffed with a conviction of the bleffings which would arife from the fuccefs of his plans, how eafily will it vindicate to his own fatisfaction any line of conduct which he may wifh to purfue. If he be ambitious and defigning, it will never fail to fupply him with fpecious reafoning, with which he may dazzle or blind his fubjects, and prevent them from oppofing him with firmnefs and vigour.

Nor would this principle point more directly, or lead more rapidly, to civil than to religious flavery. When the matchlefs benefits of true faith, and the invaluable happinefs of everlafting falvation, were preffed upon him, how often would an [a] upright monarch

[a] Mr. Paley allows (P. 328, Vol. II.) that, if fuch conclufions as thefe would follow from his principle, it muft be given up. In fact it muft, according to his own ftatement, be given up, if it be probable that fuch conduct, as thofe conclufions profefs to authorife, would frequently follow from its reception. He ftates, in perfect conformity to his principles (P. 329), that it is lawful for the magiftrate to interfere in the affairs of religion, *whenever* his interference

narch be perfuaded that general expediency required him to abandon the heretic to the zeal of the mifguided, but well-meaning, prieft? And how much more frequently would the tyrant and the bigot defend upon this plea the preconcerted facrifice of an obnoxious fect to their rapacity and pride?

A moderate knowledge of hiftory will teach us that this reafoning is confirmed by numerous facts. The principle of expediency has been alleged to juftify fucceffive invafions of the civil and religious rights of mankind, too palpably unjuft to be vindicated on any other plea. Was it not alleged when the Albigenfes were devoted to the fword, when the fires of the Inquifition were kindled? Unhappily for the world, its influence is not extinguifhed in modern times. Was it not the foundation of the abominable doctrines of the Jefuits, of their intriguing counfels as politicians, their unchriftian compliances as miffionaries? Have we not recently heard

interference *appears to him* to conduce by its general tendency to the public happinefs. Will not fuch an appearance continually prefent itfelf to the eye of ignorance, of policy, and of enthufiafm?

it

it maintained to vindicate the actions of a neighbouring despotic monarch; and those of a subject frequently more despotic, the West Indian planter?

I have selected the foregoing examples of the probable effects of the reception of this rule, as being capable, from their magnitude, of description and illustration; but perhaps I should be justified in affirming that the numberless train of evils which would spring from the same source, and infest private life, though singly not sufficiently prominent to be characterised, would collectively produce an aggregate of misery greater than all that could arise from the instances which I have produced.

Upon inquiry, I believe it will be found that few systems of oppression have not been justified or palliated on the principle laid down by Mr. Paley.

I will conclude these remarks with submitting two considerations to the judgment of the reader:

Firſt, Does it appear probable, *a priori*, that the Almighty would leave his creatures to the guidance of ſo vague and ſo dangerous a rule?

Secondly, If an unprejudiced perſon were to argue from general expediency alone, would not his firſt concluſion be, that this rule of conduct ſhould not be adopted by men?

CHAP. IV.

ARGUMENTS AGAINST THE TRUTH OF MR. PALEY'S PRINCIPLE, DEDUCED FROM A COMPARISON OF THAT PRINCIPLE WITH THE SCRIPTURES.

I SHALL in the next place examine what countenance Mr. Paley's principle of general expediency derives from the fcriptures.

The firſt confideration which will ſtrike an attentive mind is the total filence of the Old and New Teſtament on the fubject. * In no part whatever of holy writ are we directed to frame our conduct in obedience to this rule. The inſtructions therein contained are, like the duties which they enforce, of two kinds; fome are precife and abſolute, as the injunc-

* The injunction " to do good unto all men" will fcarcely be alleged as a fcriptural proof of Mr. Paley's principle. Taken in the moſt comprehenfive fenfe, it does not command or encourage us, in doing good, to follow our ideas of general expediency, in oppofition to the directions of holy writ.

tions prohibiting idolatry, perjury, and various crimes; others, equally obligatory, are indeterminate, as the precepts enjoining reverence of parents and charity to the poor. With regard to the performance of duties of the firſt claſs, no ſcope is given for the exerciſe of human diſcretion, no deviation allowed from a conſideration of the conſequences of obeying; man is peremptorily commanded to abſtain from the forbidden act. As to the others, though in general we are left to judge of the manner in which they are to be diſcharged, yet it by no means appears that our determination is to be governed by the principle ſtated by Mr. Paley. It will be ſhewn hereafter that this cannot be ſuppoſed to have been in any caſe intended by our Maker. We are indeed directed, whatever we do, to do it for the glory of God; but it remains to be proved that we ſhall promote the glory of God by purſuing our notions of general expediency.

The ſilence of the ſcriptures is not the only nor the ſtrongeſt reaſon we have for concluding that Mr. Paley's principle is inconſiſtent with our obedience to God. Revelation

lation admits of no agreement or parley with a doctrine utterly subversive of the spirit and obligation of her precepts. The statement of Mr. Paley's positions, which I have given in the second chapter, together with some of the remarks made upon them in the third, affords incontestable proof, that in his opinion there is no command in holy writ, however plainly expressed, however forcibly inculcated, which a man is not permitted, which he is not bound, to violate, whenever his blindness, his interest, his frenzy, induce him to imagine that the violation will ultimately be productive of advantage. Every man is thus invested with an unlimitted dispensing power, authorising him to take the government out of the hands of God, and to decide when his laws are proper, and when they are not proper, to be obeyed! Such a dispensing power has not hitherto been admitted among protestants; and it is as little to be tolerated, and as little to be justified, on the plea of general expediency, as on that of infallibility. Mr. Paley observes concerning honour what he might with no less truth have affirmed of general expediency, that " if its unautho-
" rised

"rifed laws [b] be allowed to create exceptions to divine prohibitions, there is an end of all morality as founded on the will of the Deity; and the obligation of every duty may at one time or other be difcharged by the caprice and fluctuation of fafhion," and the fuggeftions of felfifh ignorance.

It may not be ufelefs to produce one of the inftances in Mr. Paley's work, in which an adherence to his principle has led him to conclufions at variance with the fcriptures.

In his chapter entitled " The confideration of general confequences purfued" we meet with the following lines : " From the principles delivered in this and the two preceding chapters, a maxim may be explained, which is in every man's mouth, and in moft men's without meaning; viz. *not to do evil that good may come* — that is, let us not violate a general rule for the fake of any *particular* good confequences we may expect—which is *for the moſt part* a falutary caution, the advantage *ſeldom*

[b] P. 273, Vol. I.

" com-

" compenfating for the violation of the
" rule."

This explanation of the precept is no lefs circumfcribed than the permiffion of difcretional exceptions is unauthorifed. When St. Paul rejects totally and with abhorrence the doctrine of doing evil that good may come, and affirms of thofe who falfely imputed it to him, that their damnation is juft; on what fcriptural grounds can it be called by fo light a name as a caution? On what fcriptural grounds can it be inferred, that the opinion which we may entertain of future confequences, whether particular or general, will in any cafe abfolve us from obedience ^e? Let the reader fairly put a cafe to himfelf: let him fuppofe that it were in his power to obtain the management of a great empire by means of perfidy and murder; and that he were perfuaded that the confequences of his taking thofe previous fteps would be on the

---

^e In the fubfequent chapter I apprehend it will be proved that there is as little ground furnifhed by *reafon* for applying general expediency as the criterion of this or of any moral rule.

whole

whole beneficial to mankind—would he then take them? Would he liften to the tempter who fuggefts to him, "*" All thefe things will I give thee if thou wilt fall down and worfhip me?"

The afferter of Mr. Paley's fyftem maintains that he ought.

"ᶜ Nay but, O man, who art thou that replieft againft God?"

† Matt. iv. 9. *ᵉ Rom. ix. 20.*

CHAP.

CHAP. V.

DEMONSTRATIVE REFUTATION OF MR. PALEY'S PRINCIPLE FROM REASON.

In order to prove that general expediency is the ſtandard by which men are to regulate their moral conduct, Mr. Paley obſerves, that " God Almighty wills and wiſhes the " happineſs of his creatures; and conſe- " quently that thoſe actions, which promote " that will and wiſh, muſt be agreeable to " him; and the contrary."

The fact on which his argument reſts demands our unconditional aſſent. We know that the Divine Author of the univerſe is a Being of unbounded benevolence. We know that a deſire of promoting happineſs, or, in other words, general expediency, extending to all created beings, is an unchangeable motive of his conduct. The concluſion deduced from this fact is alſo ſtrictly true. The Almighty approves or diſapproves of actions in

the

the abstract, according as they promote or impair general happiness. But many circumstances are to be taken into the accounts before we can be authorised to conclude that we then best promote universal happiness, when, according to *our ideas of it*, we appear to do so; or that the general scheme of Providence was designed to be the object of human imitation.

Are we to assume, as a self-evident proposition, that the path marked by the steps of Omnipotence is the tract in which weakness and frailty are to tread? Does it admit of no doubt, whether the principle which gives birth to the decrees of eternal wisdom be the ground on which short-sighted ignorance may best found its conclusions? Does the infinite distance between the Creator and the created afford no room for apprehension that the endless chain of causes and effects, however naked and open to the eye of God, may afford only a bewildering and delusive light to the faculties of man?

On another occasion Mr. Paley shews himself sufficiently aware that the general rule

rule by which the difpenfations of the Almighty are directed cannot be adopted as the guide of human actions. In his chapter on crimes and punifhments, after ftating that the object of the Deity in the infliction of the latter is exactly to proportion the degree of pain to the guilt of the offender, and of men, merely to prevent crimes, without regard to any fuch proportion; he remarks, (P. 273, Vol. II.) that " it is natural to
" demand the reafon why a different mea-
" fure of punifhment fhould be expected
" from God, and obferved by man; why
" that rule, which befits the abfolute and
" perfect juftice of the Deity, fhould not be
" the rule which ought to be purfued and
" imitated by human laws. The folution of
" this difficulty muft be fought for *in thofe*
" *peculiar attributes of the divine nature*,
" which diftinguifh the difpenfations of fu-
" preme wifdom from the proceedings of
" human judicature. A Being, whofe know-
" ledge penetrates every concealment; from
" the operation of whofe will no art or flight
" can efcape; and in whofe hands punifh-
" ment is fure; fuch a Being may conduct
" the moral government of his creation, in
" the

" the best and wisest manner, by pronouncing
" a law that every crime shall finally receive
" a punishment proportioned to the guilt
" which it contains, abstracted from any fo-
" reign consideration whatever; and may
" testify his veracity to the spectators of his
" judgments, by carrying this law into strict
" execution. But, when the care of the
" public safety is intrusted to men, whose
" authority over their fellow-creatures is li-
" mited by defects of power and knowledge;
" from whose utmost vigilance and sagacity
" the greatest offenders often lie hid; whose
" wisest precautions and speediest pursuit may
" be eluded by artifice or concealment; a
" *different necessity, a new rule, of proceeding*
" *results from the very imperfection of their*
" *faculties.*"

Now the divine rule of inflicting punishments comes recommended to us by the conduct of the Almighty, the same sanction on which the rule of general expediency is proposed. Had Mr. Paley employed with respect to the latter the same train of reasoning which he has adopted concerning the former, he could not have failed to discern that the

imperfection

imperfection of our faculties, compared with the peculiar attributes of the divine nature, proves the same neceffity for a different rule of human actions in the one cafe as in the other.

From the very principle of divine benevolence, on which Mr. Paley's doctrine of general expediency is founded, we muft be convinced that our Maker would never fubject his creatures to the guidance of a rule, which it is impoffible for them to comprehend, and confequently to obey. A moment's reflection muft teach us that fuch is the rule[a] propofed by Mr. Paley. General expediency is an inftrument not to be wielded by a mortal hand. The nature of general confequences is too comprehenfive to be embraced by human underftanding, too dark to be penetrated by human difcernment. In contemplating an

[a] " By prefuming to determine what is fit and what is beneficial, they prefuppofe more knowledge of the univerfal fyftem than man has attained; and therefore depend upon principles too complicated and extenfive for our comprehenfion; and there can be no fecurity in the confequence when the premifes are not underftood."
Dr. *Johnfon's Journey to the Weftern Ifles*, p. 253.

action, who can form any adequate judgment of its collateral and remote effects making unceasing approaches towards infinity and eternity? Yet (as Mr. Paley obferves), in computing confequences, it makes no difference in what way or at what diftance they enfue. In inftances the moft level to our capacities we perceive no more than a part of the effects which may refult from our conduct; a part perhaps which, in point either of extent or importance, bears no affignable proportion to that which remains unfeen. A faint glimpfe of particular expediency is all that can ever be attained by the wifeft of men. A view of general utility is the property of God alone; in him alone it is inherent; to created beings it may be incommunicable: but, whether communicable or not, it can never be the foundation of a rule of conduct to thofe on whom it has not been beftowed. A proof of general good, being highly difficult of inveftigation, would have rendered it improbable that mankind fhould, in all cafes, be required to confult it: a proof that it is never to be difcerned demonftrates the impoffibility of their being required to confult it in any.

But

But perhaps it will be said that I have been combating a phantom raised by myself; that Mr. Paley by no means intended to affirm that our moral conduct is to be guided by an actual view of general expediency in this comprehensive sense, that view being confessedly beyond the reach of our faculties; but that our actions are to be regulated by what appears to us to be expedient, as far as we can discern their probable consequences.

Such an explanation affords no real support to Mr. Paley's system. It is a confession that we are to look not to *general* expediency, but to an expediency extending, as we imagine, to the few, and perhaps unimportant, consequences which we can distinguish; in other words, to *particular* expediency, and that of a most limited kind. All that has been urged in the third and fourth chapters against the rule of general expediency, from its probable effects on human happiness, and from its opposition to the tenor and authority of scripture, applies with equal force against this particular expediency: this would have an equal tendency to fill the world with oppression and misery; this gives an equal right to transgress the commands of revelation at discretion.

Supposing for a moment that the last objection were not conclusive against the admission of the rule, what are the advantages which may be alleged by its advocates as inducements for its reception? Is it such a rule as would best qualify us to promote the divine plan of universal good? Is the degree of expediency, which we can discern, in any case such as to justify us in inferring that we have a tolerable insight into general expediency? Surely no one will answer in the affirmative. As well might an Abyssinian pretend to delineate the whole course of the Nile, in consequence of having traced the windings of the infant river for a few miles contiguous to his hut. As well might a fisherman infer that his line, which has reached the bottom of the creek in which he exercises his trade, is capable of fathoming the depths of the Atlantic. He, who best knows how few are the consequences which he can foresee, compared with those which are

wrapped

wrapped in obscurity, will be the most ready to confess his ignorance of the universal effects of his actions.

If this argument wanted confirmation, it might receive it from a view of the moral, to say nothing of the natural, government of the world. Even though we are previously convinced that the great object of the Almighty is the happiness of his creatures, in numerous instances we see very imperfectly how the detail of his operations conduces to the end which he has in view. Sometimes presumptuous ignorance would lead us to imagine that we perceive circumstances which militate against it—as the permission of moral evil; others wherein there is an appearance of imperfection—as in the late establishment and partial diffusion of Christianity; and numbers which seem indifferent to the design proposed, or neither fully nor directly to conduce to it. If then we are so far from discovering the propriety and excellence of the parts of a system, which we are certain is framed in exact conformity to the standard of general expediency, we may be convinced how little our utmost sagacity could have discovered of the ultimate tendency and effects of our conduct; we may be assured that we are wholly unqualified to determine whether those actions, which seem to further the particular expediency within the reach of our foresight, would or would not conduce to general good; that the limited knowledge of expediency attainable by the wisest of men is unfit to be adopted as the basis of moral rectitude; and that, if it were adopted, we should too often be acting in direct opposition to the will of God, at the time when [b] we had fondly persuaded ourselves that we were most strenuously employed in promoting it.

If a pilot were entangled among quicksands, and overtaken by a fog, would he disregard his compass and his chart, depending on the strength of his eyesight alone for security from surrounding dangers, and for a safe arrival at the distant harbour? If a Christian find himself involved in temptations and difficulties, should he rely on his very contracted views of expediency, in opposition to

[b] This has particularly been the case with religious persecutors, but by no means with them alone.

the

the dictates of the gospel? Yet sooner may that pilot have a clear insight into the remotest and darkest recesses of the ocean than the Christian into the indefinite consequences of his actions. The pilot is concerned to judge aright, that he may escape present death; the Christian, that he may secure himself from death eternal.

These arguments, together with those contained in the third and fourth chapters, seem to form an insuperable barrier against the admission of this rule of particular utility, on whatever foundations it may be represented as fixed. It cannot however be in any degree fixed on the foundation upon which Mr. Paley's argument in behalf of his principle avowedly rests; for it cannot be collected from the conduct of God. Our knowledge of the attributes of the Deity enables us to assert his universal benevolence; but our experience of his dispensations by no means permits us to affirm that he always thinks fit to act in such a manner as is productive of particular expediency; much less to conclude that he wills us always to act in such a manner as we suppose would be productive of it.

it. This appears sufficiently plain from what has been already stated; but here revelation comes to the aid of reason, and precludes all further argument on this subject. Scripture abounds with instances of evils brought, as it is there declared, by the hand of the Almighty on individuals and on nations for their ultimate benefit. Nor has our heavenly Father adopted a different conduct under the Christian dispensation. We know that he wishes the happiness of each individual; yet how often does he inflict on his faithful servant a particular calamity, the disappointment of promising hopes, bodily distempers, mental disability? Who would think himself authorised by his views of expediency in inflicting these, or similar calamities? But in the hands of the Almighty occasional evil is frequently employed, how frequently we know not, as an instrument of producing general good: as the drug, which in its own nature contains a deadly poison, under the management of the skilful physician becomes a salutary remedy. General good we can affirm to be the uniform object of the divine conduct; particular good we can discern not to be that object. Consequently, whatever reason we might have for conceiving

conceiving that we should be bound by the will of God to an invariable pursuit of the former object, if we were able to discern it, we can have none for concluding that he wills the latter to be the fixed criterion of our moral conduct.

The remarks contained in the present and the two preceding chapters have finally brought us to this conclusion.

The conduct of the Almighty affords us no ground for inferring that he wills us to conform our moral actions to the standard assumed by Mr. Paley, whether that standard be our opinion of *general* or of *particular* expediency. Reason rejects the former principle as beyond her comprehension, and both of them as subversive of human happiness; and revelation forbids us to listen to doctrines, either of which arms every man with a discretionary power of violating her most sacred laws.

PART

PART II.

GENERAL RIGHTS AND OBLIGATIONS OF MEN, DEDUCED FROM REASON AND REVELATION.

CHAP. I.

PRELIMINARY REMARKS ON THE GROUNDS FROM WHICH THE PRINCIPLES OF HUMAN CONDUCT ARE TO BE DERIVED BY NATURAL REASON—STATEMENT OF CERTAIN PRINCIPLES.

IF it has been demonstrated in the former part of this treatise that general expediency is not the principle from which reason is to deduce moral conclusions, the question will immediately arise, on what grounds is she to proceed?

A recollection of the erroneous and fatal inferences, which we have seen would naturally be derived from a principle lost in remotenefs

motenefs and obfcurity, will contribute materially to facilitate our refearches. It will convince us that the utility of the premifes, from which rules of life are to be drawn, depends on their not taking their rife from too high a fource, and on their being accommodated, as much as may be, to the general level of human capacity. From a view of the fituation and nature of man; a being placed on this earth by his Maker, endowed by him with peculiar gifts, and accountable to him for the ufe of them; a number of fubordinate rules may, I apprehend, be deduced adequate to the purpofe of directing his fteps in every cafe on which the gofpel is filent; rules which will not only appear to be fanctioned by the uniform tenor of revelation, but in return will fupport and corroborate the injunctions of holy writ.

Mr. Paley having remarked that the will of God, the invariable ftandard of our conduct, is, in the firft place, to be fought in fcripture; and, if it cannot be difcovered therein, is, in the next place, to be collected from general expediency, illluftrates his obfervations by the following inftance:
"An

" *An ambassador, judging by what he
" knows of his sovereign's disposition, and
" arguing from what he has observed of his
" conduct, or is acquainted with of his de-
" signs, may take his measures in many
" cases with safety; and presume with great
" probability how his master would have him
" act on most occasions that arise: but,
" if he have his commission and instructions
" in his pocket, it would be strange not to
" look into them. He will naturally con-
" duct himself by both rules: when his in-
" structions are clear and positive, there is an
" end of all further deliberation (unless indeed
" he suspect their authenticity): where his
" instructions are silent or dubious, he will
" endeavour to supply or explain them by
" what he has been able to collect from other
" quarters of his master's general inclination
" or intentions."

Where the ambassador's instructions are clear, without doubt he will implicitly obey them: where they are silent, or afford but ambiguous light, he is not to substitute in their place his own ideas of what may be ge-

* P. 63, Vol. I.

nerally

nerally expedient for his country. He knows that his mafter's uniform defign is to promote the general good of the empire; that defign he is bound to further, but not by immediately taking upon himfelf to judge what circumftances will be moft beneficial. He previoufly fixes his attention on a number of fubordinate particulars, which may fupply the deficiency of his inftructions, by giving him precife indications of the line of conduct which he ought to adopt. He reflects that his mafter has uniformly oppofed the opening of this port, the impofition of this duty, and the repair of that fortrefs. To thefe points, though omitted in his inftructions, and to all points clearly analogous to them, he rigidly adheres; he depends on their being generally expedient for the empire, perhaps he difcerns them to be fo; but, if he is unable to difcover this, if he imagines that he fees fome appearance of the contrary, his confcience obliges him uniformly to infift upon propofitions which his reafon tells him are enjoined by the will of his fovereign.

When a Chriftian receives ambiguous inftructions, or no inftructions, from his gofpel, let him not extend his view to
a fubject

a subject which can be contemplated only by an infinite mind; let him, like the ambassador, consider his own peculiar situation; let him endeavour to collect the will of his sovereign on some specific and fundamental points; and, from the result of his inquiry, deduce subordinate rules for the direction of his conduct. There is another circumstance to be taken into the account:— the ambassador may feel assured that his master is mistaken, the Christian will not deem the same of his.

Research into the original rights and obligations of unconnected individuals must necessarily precede all inquiries into the duties of men when united in civil society. For the only objects, the disposal and arrangement of which can be claimed by any society, are the respective rights of its several members. The materials therefore must be collected before the fabric can be raised.

A reference to these rights and obligations must also regulate the conduct of the members of the same society towards each other, in all cases, when the laws of the society do not give precise directions.

And

And a fimilar reference muft govern their behaviour towards all individuals not belonging to their fociety, nor connected with it by any exprefs or implied engagements.

I fhall, therefore, in the firft place, inveftigate the primitive rights and obligations of mankind independent of the fcriptures, and of the inftitution of civil fociety; and fhall afterwards point out how far they are confirmed by the former, and on what principle they may be fufpended or modified by the latter.

For this purpofe I fhall endeavour to prove the truth of the following propofitions.

> I. Every man has originally a right, by the gift of God, to the unreftrained enjoyment of life and perfonal freedom; and to fuch a portion of the unappropriated productions of the earth as is neceffary for his comfortable fubfiftence.

> II. He therefore, who deprives another of thefe gifts, or reftrains him in the enjoyment of them, except fuch deprivation

ation or restraint is sanctioned by divine authority, is guilty of an act of injustice to the individual, and of a sin against God.

III. Every man originally has authority from God to deprive another of these gifts, or to restrain him in the enjoyment of them in the following cases, and in those only:

1st, When in so doing he acts according to the express command of God.

2dly, When he proceeds in such deprivation and restraint so far, and so far only, as is necessary for the defence of the gifts of God to himself, or, in case his assistance is desired, in defence of the gifts of God to another, against attacks unauthorised by God.

3dly, When he proceeds to such deprivation or restraint in consequence of the consent of the individual suffering it.

IV. Every

IV. Every man sins against God who either voluntarily consents to relinquish or abridge any of his natural rights; or who does not endeavour to resist, by all requisite force, every unauthorised invasion of them, except he is persuaded that, by imposing the restraints in question upon himself, or by submitting to the imposition of them by another, he shall not in any degree disqualify himself from answering, on the whole, the great purposes of his being. And in like manner every man sins against God who accepts from another a transfer of any of his rights, unless he is persuaded that by such acceptance he shall not in any degree disqualify the latter from answering, on the whole, the great purposes of his being.

If these propositions shall be satisfactorily established, they will be found to settle on solid and determinate grounds the obligations of justice in all its branches; and to afford a clear insight into the distinguishing characteristics of what moralists have usually styled perfect and imperfect rights.

CHAP. II.

THE FIRST AND SECOND PROPOSITIONS DEMONSTRATED.

The first proposition to be proved is, that "every man has originally a right, by the gift of God, to the unrestrained enjoyment of life and personal freedom; and to such a portion of the unappropriated productions of the earth as is necessary for his comfortable subsistence."

By the terms personal freedom, I must always be understood to mean freedom from personal injury as well as from personal restraint.

By a right, I mean authority from God for the enjoyment of any particular thing, or for the performance of any particular action.

I shall also occasionally use the term right, after the example of others, to signify what

in

in strict propriety is the object of the right—as when it is said that life is one of the rights of man.

Under the expression natural rights, those rights which every individual possesses independent of the institutions of civil society, will hereafter be comprehended.

Independent of any social engagement with others of his species, every man finds himself possessed of existence, of various bodily powers and mental faculties. He cannot but discover the impossibility of his having conferred life upon himself; and must become convinced that he has received these gifts from a gracious Being, the author of himself and of the universe. He may therefore be assured that he has a right to the undisturbed enjoyment of these blessings as long as it shall seem meet to the power who bestowed them. As the wisdom apparent in the visible constitution of nature forbids him to think that the Deity would exert his power in vain, and lavish his bounty without having an adequate end in view, he may reasonably conclude that whatever has been conferred on himself has been

been conferred for important purposes. When he casts his eyes around on the rest of his species, he perceives that every individual is placed in the same situation, each possessed of life and various powers, the gifts of the same God, for purposes equally important. The same reasoning therefore may be applied in favour of their rights as in favour of their own ; and, if he applies it, he must discover it to be his duty not to incur the guilt of disobedience in the eyes of an Almighty Benefactor, and the punishment attending his displeasure, by an uncommissioned encroachment on his gifts to others ; he must know that he has no authority to interrupt any of his fellow-creatures in accomplishing those purposes, whatever they may be, for which their common Maker called them into being.

He discovers, further, that he is in danger of speedily losing all these gifts, unless he takes proper measures for their preservation. The natural want of food, and the presence of fruits capable of supplying it, afford him sufficient grounds for concluding that they were formed for the support of his life, and that he has a right to apply them to the use for which

which they were evidently intended by the will of God. And in general, perceiving how admirably different parts of the inanimate creation (which; being incapable of sensation, must be incapable of injury) answer his purposes, he may very reasonably infer that God designed them for the use of man, and may take in consequence whatever he finds necessary, whether it be for food, for raiment, for shelter, or defence. He observes too that the rest of mankind have the same wants with himself, and the same title to the objects by which they are to be removed. From these reflections he may justly determine, that the fruit which any individual has plucked from the bough, and the tree which he has felled in the forest, are the especial gifts of God to that individual; and consequently that neither has he himself any more right to interrupt another, or another to interrupt him, in the quiet enjoyment of these or any similar gifts, than either of them would have to disturb the other in the possession of life or freedom[a].

I have

---

[a] If the foregoing observations do not prove (besides their professed object) that reason might convince mankind

I have said that a man in a state of nature *might* arrive at a knowledge of his duty by the foregoing train of reasoning. Whether he *would* thus attain that knowledge, whether these several arguments and conclusions (though all of them within the reach of his faculties, and some of them most obvious) would in reality suggest themselves to his mind, is a point of no importance to the present inquiry. The object of our investigation is not to discover what principles he would be likely to adopt, but what principles he ought to adopt. An acquaintance with the former might shew what his conduct probably would be; a knowledge of the latter alone can point out what it ought to be. However ignorance, prejudice, and passion, might bias and warp his opinions, they cannot alter the essential difference between right and wrong. To display this difference, to develope the rules of human duty, and place them on their true

---

kind of the existence of the Deity, and of the certainty of future rewards and punishments, I must be understood for the present to take those points for granted; as I fully agree with Mr. Paley that such a conviction is the only adequate ground of moral obligation.

foundations,

foundations, is the proper and the only business of the moralist.

The first proposition being established, it will follow, as it is expressed in the second, that he who deprives another of the abovementioned gifts, or restrains him in the enjoyment of them, except such deprivation or restraint is sanctioned by divine authority, is guilty of an act of injustice to the individual, and of a sin against God.

We have seen that the natural title of each individual to the quiet enjoyment of life, of personal freedom, and of such a portion of the unappropriated productions of the earth as is necessary for his comfortable sustsistence, is clear, and full, resting on the will of God. A gift conferred by any authority cannot be revoked but by equal authority, or by greater. He, therefore, who claims a right forcibly to deprive his neighbour in any respect of the free use of the gifts which God has bestowed upon him, is bound to produce at least as strong and as authentic testimony of its being the will of God that the deprivation should take place, or the restraint be imposed, as the other

other can that it should not. And if he presumes, without the production of such testimony, forcibly to interfere with the rights of another, he is not only guilty of injustice to that individual, but he acts in direct defiance of the Being by whom those rights were bestowed.

No plea therefore can justify the invasion of the natural rights of another except manifest authority from God.

It remains to be considered in what cases such authority can be proved.

CHAP. III.

THE THIRD PROPOSITION DEMONSTRATED.

The first branch of the third proposition declares, that every man has originally divine authority to deprive another of the gifts of God, or to restrain him in the enjoyment of them, when in so doing he acts according to the express command of God.

It is not necessary to enlarge on a position, the truth of which no man will dispute. The reality of such a command is the only point which can ever be questioned: and we may safely determine that no claim to inspiration is to be admitted, unless it be supported by the evidence of supernatural powers; for these are the only credentials by which the inspired messenger of God can be distinguished from the impostor; and they are the credentials by which the mission of those who have been charged with especial commands from above has in all ages been authenticated.

The

The second branch of the proposition affirms, that every man has originally divine authority to deprive another of the gifts of God, or to restrain him in the enjoyment of them, when he proceeds in such deprivation or restraint so far, and so far only, as is necessary for the defence of the gifts of God to himself, or, in case his assistance is desired, in defence of the gifts of God to another, against attacks unauthorised by God.

It has been shewn, without any reference to scripture, that all men are naturally possessed of certain rights; and further, that an uncommissioned attack on the rights of another would be a sin against God.

This will be confessed. But perhaps it may be alleged, that these considerations alone do not prove our actual right of opposing by force any such attack; that restraining the freedom, and much more endangering the life of another, though an aggressor, may be a line of conduct equally unauthorised with his own; that his guilt will be no justification of ours; that we have no more right to kill an assassin than we have to destroy an infectious person,

perſon, who may be as likely to occcaſion our death; that we may lament the approach of either as a ſevere misfortune; but that it may be our duty patiently to ſubmit the event to God, and to leave to him the puniſhment of the offender, and the vindication of his own authority.

This fundamental objection to the right of ſelf-defence is not to be obviated merely by urging that the deſtruction of the human race would be the ultimate conſequence of admitting it. We are not allowed to oppoſe our ideas of future conſequences to the direct authority of God. It has been proved that every man has originally that authority for the quiet enjoyment of his natural rights; and we muſt produce authority equally direct before we preſume to reſtrain them.

In reply then it may be obſerved, that it would be no leſs our duty to guard our life againſt the infected man than againſt the aſſaſſin; and, if the former ſhould *wilfully* attempt to injure our health, he may be reſiſted by the ſame methods as the latter. If no ſuch attempt be made, ſalutary precautions or removal are the only juftifiable means of felf-prefervation; for, even if we take for granted that we fhould be authorifed to oppofe him by force if he fhould purpofely invade our rights, we can have no claim to reftrain him if he does not. A proof however of the irrelevance of a particular inftance does not invalidate the principle which it was intended to illuftrate. The fubfequent remarks, it is apprehended, directly meet and refute the objection.

The natural ability which every man has received from his Maker of retaining, abridging, or relinquifhing, any of his actual rights, as well as of accepting a transfer of the rights of others, it may be prefumed that he has authority to exert and employ, *fo far as is compatible with the gifts of God to his fellow creatures.* And this prefumption is confirmed by inconteftable arguments. The authority in queftion is neceffary to conftitute each individual a moral agent. The difcretional right of employing the gifts of God, in a manner either conformable or repugnant to the donor's will, renders his exiftence a ftate of trial, and himfelf a fit object of future retribution.

retribution. He is to accomplish, by his own endeavours, the purposes of his being; he is therefore constituted the guardian of his natural rights, by the use of which those purposes are to be accomplished; he is commissioned to judge in every case of the means requisite for the defence of the gifts committed to his custody; and is equally authorised, within the limits abovementioned, to protect them from injury, whether it be likely to arise from hunger, from cold, from the violence of a savage animal, or from the unwarranted attacks of a savage of his own species.

He, therefore, who, by unjustly invading the rights of another, has met with resistance, and has thereby lost any of his natural rights, his property, his health, his limbs, or his life, must impute the loss wholly to himself. He runs upon a weapon pointed against him by the hand of God; and the detriment which he receives is to be viewed in the same light as if it had been incurred by means of any other incident, which, by God's appointment, is attended with consequences painful or destructive.

To

To the preceding obfervations fome important inferences may be fubjoined.

Firft: The fame reafons, which prove that men are authorifed by the will of God to defend their rights when actually attacked, equally prove them to be authorifed, when they are fufficiently affured that an attack is intended by another, to lay fuch reftraints on him as are neceffary to prevent it, and to continue them fo long as that neceffity fubfifts.

Secondly: The fame reafons likewife juftify men in taking all neceffary methods to compel the reftitution of the freedom, or the property of which they have been unjuftly deprived; fuch methods being only a continuation of the refiftance which was made, or an exertion of fuch as might have been made, to the original attack. And they equally juftify the neceffary means for obtaining, what is analogous to reftitution, an equitable indemnification for fuch rights as cannot be reftored.

Thirdly: They apply equally to the defence and recovery of all the actual rights of men, whether originally received from God, or obtained

tained by their own exertions, or by the assistance and consent of others.

Fourthly: They do not authorise any manner of resistance beyond what is necessary to secure men from the effects of the violence offered to them, or impending over them.

Lastly: Whoever, by self-defence, in a case wherein self-defence was a duty, has incurred the hazard or loss of his life or other natural rights, is not chargeable with the guilt of disqualifying himself from fulfilling his Maker's purposes; the risk of such loss being inseparable from the resistance which God enjoins.

It remains to be shewn[a] under what circumstances an individual may be justified by the

---

[a] They, who maintain the existence of a *moral sense*, will rank, among its suggestions, the desire of assisting a fellow-creature in distress; and will consider that desire as an indication that a man has in all cases a natural right, by the will of God, to interpose by force in defence of the injured. However difficult it may be for my reader, whose benevolence is enlarged by revelation, to decline giving his assent to this argument, yet he will reflect, that no stress can be laid upon it until the *fact* on which it rests be

the light of nature in forcibly depriving another of his rights, by giving affiftance to a third perfon attacked by the latter.

From our former conclufions it is evident that he cannot be juftified in thus interfering in behalf of any one whom he has reafon to think may be the aggreffor; nor in any cafe in interfering further than is neceffary to fecure the rights of himfelf and of thofe whom he protects.

Under thefe limitations he may interfere;

Firft: When the defence of the injured party is by nature committed to his care; as is the cafe of a parent and his young children.

Secondly: When his affiftance is requefted by the party aggrieved; for the latter has a right to impofe the neceffary reftraints on the affailant by all the means in his power, and by his requeft imparts this right to the other.

be inconteftably eftablifhed. We are not at liberty precipitately to obey the impulfe of philanthropy, unlefs we are previoufly convinced, on higher grounds, that we have a right to act in the manner propofed.

Thirdly:

Thirdly: When his own security is immediately connected with that of the person whom he assists; as if he is himself one of a a company attacked by robbers: for the case then becomes self-defence.

Fourthly: When his own security is eventually concerned in repressing unauthorised invasions of the rights of another. And this will almost always be the case; since the safety of his own rights essentially depends on the repression of that injustice which he may reasonably expect will ere long be directed against himself, if permitted to trample on the rights of those around him.

In the last branch of the third proposition it is asserted, that every man has originally divine authority to deprive another of the gifts of God, or to restrain him in the enjoyment of them, when he proceeds to such deprivation or restraint in consequence of the consent of the individual suffering it.

This point has already been settled; as I have found it necessary in a former part of the present chapter to prove that every man is
originally

originally invested by his Maker with discretional authority to dispose of all his natural rights, and likewise to accept a transfer of the rights of another [b].

We have now, I apprehend, considered all the cases in which a man has divine authority to deprive another of the gifts of God, or to restrain him in the enjoyment of them. Should any one assert that he has this authority in a case not comprehended within the limits of those which have been discussed, he must contend, if he would render his claim worthy of serious notice, that the right has been bestowed upon him for one or more of the following purposes.

1. To enable him to promote the happiness of himself;

2. Or the happiness of the individual whose rights he is about to infringe:

[b] The cases and the manner in which these rights, and the other rights which have been established, ought to be exercised, will be investigated under the remaining proposition.

3. Or

3. Or the happiness of some other individual:

4. Or the happiness of mankind in general; in other words, for the sake of general expediency.

On the first head it will be sufficient to observe, that a claim set up by an uninspired individual to infringe the gifts of God to another, whenever he conceives that such a step will conduce to his own happiness, is an insult to him who conferred those gifts; and is resisted by the whole train of reasoning which has been employed to shew that all men possess the same natural rights, and have those rights at their own disposal. It is a claim which every one may assert, which no one can prove, and which never can be admitted until it be established by proofs the most decisive.

If, in the second place, the aggressor rest his claim on the ground of contributing to the good of the individual whose rights he is about to invade, can he shew that the Almighty has constituted him the judge of his neighbour's bour's happiness? On the contrary, is it not the fact that God has left every man to determine what line of conduct will most effectually promote his own welfare; and has empowered him to act accordingly, provided that he does not thereby infringe the rights of any of his fellow-creatures? Nay, hath it not been shewn essential to moral agency, that every one, who is to be rewarded or punished for the use he shall make of the gifts which God has bestowed upon him, should have the power of employing them in any manner which he shall think most conducive to his happiness, subject only to the abovementioned limitation, and of retaining or relinquishing them solely at his own option? It follows then, that, even if the assailant could prove by the most incontestable evidence that the happiness of the person whom he attacks would be in the highest degree promoted by the loss of the rights in question, such a proof would contribute nothing to his own vindication. What though we admit it to be on this account the duty of the other in the sight of God to resign them; it is a duty, for the discharge of which he is answerable only to his God!—for it is the possessor of these rights, and not the

invader

invader of them, whom God has appointed to judge in what cafes it is more advifable that they fhould be retained, and when it is better that they fhould be relinquifhed.

Thirdly: If the aggreffor maintain his claim on the ground of promoting the happinefs, not of the perfon attacked, but of fome other individual, or individuals, an application of the preceding obfervations will fhew that a prefumption, or a conviction, of what their happinefs requires, will not in any degree juftify his invafion of the rights of another. If he has no authority to impofe reftraints, in order that he may promote the happinefs of the perfon reftrained, a claim to impofe them for the benefit of others muft be, if poffible, more unreafonable.

The fourth plea, that of general expediency, has been, I apprehend, fo fully refuted in the former part of this treatife, that it may be difmiffed without further difcuffion.

It may not be improper in this place to inquire whether reftraints, the original impofition

fition of which was unjuftifiable, may in any cafes be continued confiftently with juftice.

The principles laid down in the prefent chapter evidently point out the following rule. Reftraints originally unjuft may be continued in all cafes which would juftify the prefent impofition of them, and in no other.

Thus, if I had unjuftifiably taken a fword from another man, I fhould be authorifed to retain it fo long as I fhould have fufficient reafon to believe that, on receiving it, he would revenge himfelf by plunging it in my breaft. After the fatisfaction of his claims, and the removal of his apprehenfions, he would have no grounds for reftraining me in the enjoyment of my natural rights; and I fhould be juftified in the previous ufe of all neceffary force to fecure myfelf from a meditated injury.

I will fubjoin another inftance, though drawn from civil fociety, a fubject which has not yet been inveftigated, as it relates to a topic much agitated at prefent. The Weft-Indian

negroes,

negroes, though in general reduced to slavery by unjust means, may be detained in that state as long as there is sufficient reason to believe that, if emancipated, they would massacre the planters, or ravage the islands.

In all cases however the foregoing rule presupposes that it is full and impartial deliberation which has convinced us that the continuance of the restraint in question is necessary to our justifiable self-defence: for otherwise we should not be authorised now to impose it.

If, for example, methods can be devised, and I see no reason why they may not, which may enable us to emancipate the children of the negroes without exposing our colonies to the abovementioned calamities, we are bound in justice to adopt them. Nor can we be authorised to continue the unjust slavery, either of children or parents, unless a *serious* and *candid* inquiry convinces us that no such means are to be found.

It must be observed that the principles, which have been maintained respecting self-defence and refiftance, apply to men fo far only as nature conftitutes them moral agents. Thus they do not interfere with the natural rights of parents over their children; nor do they prohibit the exercife of falutary force towards a lunatic or an idiot; nor, on the proper occafions, towards thofe who are incidentally difordered in their underftanding.

CHAP.

CHAP. IV.

THE FOURTH PROPOSITION DEMONSTRATED.

A principal object of the preceding propositions has been to ascertain those actions, which, antecedently to the institution of society, would not only be sins against God, but would also be acts of injustice to men. The actions noticed in the following proposition are such as would be offences in the sight of God, although not acts of injustice to any individual.

The fourth proposition is as follows:

Every man sins against God, who either voluntarily consents to relinquish or abridge any of his natural rights, or who does not endeavour to resist by all requisite force every unauthorised invasion of them; except he is persuaded that, by imposing the restraints in question upon himself, or by submitting to the imposition of them by another, he shall
not

not in any degree difqualify himfelf from anfwering on the whole the great purpofes of his being. And in like manner every man fins againft God, who accepts from another a transfer of any of his rights, unlefs he is perfuaded that by fuch acceptance he fhall not in any degree difqualify the latter from anfwering on the whole the great purpofes of his being.

Since it is obvious that every particular reftraint, whether partial or total, of the exercife of any natural right, which an individual cannot impofe upon himfelf without offending God, it is his duty to refift when an attempt to impofe it is made by another; it will be the moft fimple, and at the fame time no unfatisfactory method of difcuffing the firft part of the propofition, to confine our demonftration to that part of it which refpects the duty of refiftance or forbearance.

It is the natural duty of every man to endeavour to preferve himfelf in fuch a ftate as may beft enable him to fulfil the will of God; or, in other words, to anfwer thofe purpofes for which his Maker called him into being.
And,

And, since almighty wisdom bestows no gift but for an end adequate to the value of that gift, there is in every case a presumption, antecedent to reasonings on either side of the question, that each right, of which an individual finds himself possessed by the bounty of Providence, is necessary to enable him fully to accomplish the purposes of his existence; and consequently that God wills him to retain it. He therefore sins against God if he slights this presumption, and forbears from resisting to the utmost of his power by all requisite force every invasion of his rights; unless he is convinced, by a full and impartial consideration of the benefits likely to result from his forbearance as well as from his resistance, that the former measure will upon the whole conduce at least as much as the latter to the ends for which he was created. If his conclusion should be, that the whole or the more important of these ends will be most effectually promoted by forbearance, it is then no less his duty to forbear, than it would have been on the contrary supposition to resist.

Similar considerations will also teach him whether he ought or ought not voluntarily to abridge

abridge or to relinquish the exercise of any of his uninvaded rights.

It follows, from the observations which have been made, that he, who resists in a case wherein he conceives that his duty to God requires him to abstain from self-defence, though not answerable to the aggressor for the detriment which the latter brings upon himself by his attack, is answerable for it to his Maker; and also for the injury which he himself receives in the contest.

To a more severe account may he expect to be called, for the injury sustained both by himself and by the assailant, who resists when self-defence constitutes him an aggressor; as the robber, who by force withholds from its owner the property which he has stolen.

With respect to the second branch of the proposition, it is to be observed that he, who accepts from another a power of restraining any of his rights, when he has reason to believe that by such acceptance he in any degree disqualifies the other from fulfilling on the whole the purposes of his being, though he is not
answerable

answerable to the latter for the loss which he incurs by the surrender, commits a sin in the sight of God; for it is the will of God, that every one of his creatures should accomplish the ends for which he was made: he therefore is guilty of resisting that will, who knowingly contributes to disable his incautious neighbour from fulfilling it.

Since it highly concerns every individual to form in each case a rational judgment, whether his duty to God requires him voluntarily to surrender any of his rights, to defend them when invaded, or to accept or refuse a power over the rights of another; he ought previously to impress upon his mind adequate ideas of the various purposes for which he was created, and to appreciate, as far as may be, their relative importance.

The primary end of his being he knows to be the promoting and securing of his own salvation by a zealous service of his Maker.

There are subordinate purposes, conducive also to this principal object, which his reason and the very frame and constitution of his

nature

nature teach him that he was formed to answer. These are, promoting the salvation of his fellow-creatures, and their present happiness as well, as his own.

The duties which he owes to mankind in general he will perceive to be owing in different degrees to different individuals. In proportion as particular persons are more closely connected with him by the ties of kindred and of affection; in proportion as they have heretofore shewn kindness to himself; in proportion as they stand more in need of the assistance which it is in his power to bestow; in proportion to the force of any or of all these circumstances, and of others which might be enumerated, he will find himself under a more pressing obligation to promote their present and future welfare. Though he is not answerable to men if he refuses to confer upon them those benefits, which he has a discretionary power of bestowing or withholding, he is accountable for that refusal to his God. For every opportunity of doing good to one of his fellow-creatures is an opportunity afforded him by his Maker of promoting his own salvation; and he is bound by every consideration

sideration of duty never to neglect that primary end of his existence.

The deduction of a few examples from the positions which have been maintained in this chapter may throw a clearer light on the subject.

Every man is bound in the sight of God to resist, if an attempt be made to deprive him of the liberty of praying to or praising God: for his own salvation is the primary end of his being, and those are his primary duties which must form the basis of the intercourse between himself and his Maker.

For the same reasons he cannot innocently consent to renounce these rights.

Nor can he innocently accept the surrender of them from another.

But every man may innocently refrain from defending or reclaiming any part of his property, if he believes that he shall promote the whole or the more valuable of his Maker's purposes

purposes equally well by forbearance as by resistance; and he ought to refrain, if he believes that he shall thus promote them better.

Similar considerations may prove that he is at liberty, or that he is obliged, in the sight of God, to accept from another a power over his property; supposing him to believe that neither the latter by parting with it, nor himself by accepting it, will answer less effectually the whole or the more valuable of the respective purposes of their being.

CHAP.

CHAP. V.

THE PRECEDING PROPOSITIONS SHEWN TO BE CONFIRMED BY THE SCRIPTURES.

The principles, which have been deduced in the three preceding chapters from the light of unassisted reason, will acquire much additional authority, if they are shewn to be sanctioned by the scriptures. I shall, therefore, briefly prove that they possess this sanction, before I proceed to derive from them any further conclusions.

In the first place, the scriptures teach us, in concurrence with the first proposition, that existence, with every bodily power and mental faculty possessed by each individual, was bestowed upon him by the bountiful hand of God. They also declare, in general expressions, which convey the same natural rights to every individual, that the earth, under which term its various productions are manifestly comprehended, was delivered unto man to be *subdued* by him; that is, to be employed in such manner, and converted to such uses, as his necessities should require. He was invested with a particular right of applying the vegetable creation (a single exception being made, with the object of which he did not long continue to be conversant), to the purpose of his sustenance; and at a later period he received an extension [a] of his authority; an extension giving him an unlimited power over the whole animal world, which already to a certain degree had been subjected to his dominion.

Further: It is to be observed that the scriptures have for their principal object the inculcation of this fundamental truth—that every man is placed upon earth by his Maker to work out his salvation by his own actions.

[a] As animals are evidently susceptible of pain and injury, man, uninstructed by revelation, could not have had the least right to exercise any authority over them. To restrain them in the enjoyment, much more to deprive them of the possession, of those gifts, which his and their Maker had seen it good to bestow upon them, would have been in every case, except that of self-defence, an act of usurpation, and a sin against that Power, who, for wise ends known to himself, had called them into existence.

Since the reward or punishment of every man will be increased in proportion to the manner in which he employs each of the means of action of which he is possessed, the scriptures necessarily and incontestably imply that his conduct should be free, except in cases in which it is restrained by his Maker: in other words (as it has been asserted in the second proposition), that he is guilty of a sin against God, who deprives another of any of the gifts of God, or restrains him in the enjoyment of them, except he has authority from God for so doing: and that he is also guilty of an act of injustice to the person thus deprived or restrained.

The reader will recollect that the right and duty of self-defence, the limitations to which they are subject, and all other rules of conduct laid down in the third and fourth propositions, or developed in the explanation of them, were severally rested on these principles; that each individual, being intrusted with the charge of accomplishing, by his own endeavours, the purposes of his being, must necessarily be constituted the guardian of the gifts bestowed upon him, for the use of which he he is accountable; that it is his duty to exercife the difcretional power with which he is invefted in fuch a manner as may beft enable him to fulfil the ends for which he was made; namely, to promote and fecure his own falvation, together with the falvation of others, and their prefent happinefs as well as his own. Now, fince thefe principles do ultimately coincide with the great fcriptural truth which has been ftated above, it follows that every conclufion deduced from them by fair reafoning has fcriptural authority for its bafis. For a proof that the particular conclufions which have been deduced in the two preceding chapters are confirmed by the whole tenor of fcripture, if my reader is well acquainted with his Bible, I will appeal to his own knowledge; if he is not, for the fake of obtaining this proof, among better reafons, let me requeft him to become fo.

I will dwell on this fubject no longer than while I obviate the force of a queftion which may be afked, and which fome men, I fear, would be glad to think unanfwerable: "You "have proved," it may be faid, "that the "great rules of human conduct contained in
"the

" the scriptures are discoverable by the light
" of unassisted reason.—Where then was the
" necessity for the Christian revelation?"
The Christian revelation, I reply, was necessary, that those rules of life, which none but the wisest would have deduced for themselves, and even they but imperfectly, might be placed at once before the bulk of mankind, expressed in the plainest language, founded on the most undoubted authority, and recommended by the most persuasive example. It was necessary particularly to enforce upon men the practice of the various duties of *forbearance*; a practice the most ungrateful to their natural passions. And, lastly, it was necessary to fix on immoveable foundations that corner-stone on which the whole fabric of our reasoning has been built—the certainty of a future state of retribution, in which every individual shall be rewarded or punished in exact proportion to his deeds.

CHAP. VI.

ON INDEMNIFICATION.

SEVERAL topics, which either have been curforily noticed in the foregoing chapters, or are immediately deducible from the principles which have been maintained, may not improperly receive diftinct confideration, as it is of importance that their true nature fhould be accurately underftood. The fubjects to which I allude are indemnification, punifhment, flavery, and property.

By indemnification I mean the receiving of an equivalent for an injury fuftained.

The right which an injured perfon has to indemnification, and the means by which it may be enforced, have already been fhewn in the third chapter. The manner in which the claim is to be fatisfied will appear from a review of the following cafes:

1ft: Let

1st: Let us suppose the party aggrieved to have been injured in his property alone, and the aggressor to be possessed of property sufficient for the purpose of compensation. Under these circumstances the fit mode of retribution is obvious,

2dly: But if the aggressor is destitute of property, or so poor as to be unable, even by the surrender of his whole substance, to satisfy the just demand of the man whom he has injured, how is he to complete the equivalent? He must appropriate to the use of the latter such a portion of the other gifts which God has bestowed upon him, such a portion of his strength, or of his industry, or of his skill, as will answer the remaining claim. What he cannot pay with his property he must pay with his service.

In this case, although the injured person may compel the aggressor to perform the requisite service, yet he has not necessarily a right to oblige the innocent family of the latter to co-operate in it. The aggressor, as far as he is possessed of such a right, may transfer it to the other, or may be deprived of it by him.

3dly:

3dly: Suppose the injured party to have incurred loss of time and expense in defence of his rights, or in endeavours necessary for the recovery of them.

These are so many injuries brought upon him by the wilful act of the assailant; and the sufferer has consequently a right to be indemnified. The particulars are reducible to computation, and an equivalent in property may be precisely ascertained: of course the reasoning on the foregoing cases is applicable to this.

4thly: Suppose the injured party to have undergone bodily pain or injury, or severe anxiety of mind, in consequence of the aggressor's attack.

He had originally the same right to freedom from injury in these points as in his property; and consequently has the same title to indemnification in the one case as in the other: and indemnification in these, as in all instances, must be rendered in property or in service.

It

It is evident that, in the case of unconnected individuals, where the person who had received the injury would judge of the requisite compensation, as well as enforce the discharge of it, the exercise of this right would be pushed to unwarrantable lengths, and marked with caprice, violence, and outrage. It is equally evident, that the computation of a fair equivalent would be a matter of no small difficulty even to an unprejudiced bystander. But these circumstances do not invalidate the right itself, however they may indicate the duty of moderation in the exercise of it. A right does not cease to be so because it may be abused, nor because its limits may not easily be ascertained. Yet the computer is not entirely without land-marks to direct him. He may discern this recompense to fall short of what he may fairly claim, and that to exceed it. A basket of apples would be an inadequate compensation for the loss of a finger; and a herd of oxen might be more than an equivalent. He is to discover, as nearly as may be, the just medium between the two extremes; and he is answerable to his Maker for an impartial judgment.

Indemnification

Indemnification may be demanded for the injuries sustained by the family of the party aggrieved in consequence of the attack made upon him, as far as the aggressor must reasonably be supposed to have foreseen them; for so far they must be considered as intentional injuries. This reasoning applies with still greater force where they are known to have been intended.

With respect to enforcing or waving the exercise of the right to indemnification in any particular case or degree, the injured person is bound in the sight of God to adopt that line of conduct which he apprehends will, on the whole, most effectually forward the great purposes of his being. And in forming his judgment on this point, the advantage of the aggressor, with respect to the purposes which he also was created to accomplish, will be no inconsiderable object.

CHAP. VII.

ON PUNISHMENT.

He who has obtained, by restitution or indemnification, complete satisfaction for the injuries which he has suffered, has no further claim on the aggressor, except for security against future violence, when it is on good grounds supposed to be intended. He has the same claim upon any man whom he believes to meditate an invasion of his rights, although he may never have invaded them hitherto. It has already been proved, that every man has authority from God previously to deprive another of his rights, so far as is necessary for securing himself from the proposed attacks of the latter; in other words, that every man, who has sufficient reason to believe that another individual meditates an unjust attempt against him, has a right to inflict on that individual such punishment as is necessary to prevent him from prosecuting his design.

These

These are the true and the only grounds on which the juftice of human punifhments can naturally be vindicated. To punifh, by way of inflicting vengeance for crimes already perpetrated, is to ufurp the prerogative of the Almighty.

In fome cafes fecurity cannot be attained without inflicting fuch a punifhment as abfolutely deprives the aggreffor of the power of committing the meditated outrage. In others (and thefe, fortunately for mankind, are the more numerous) the end may be fufficiently anfwered by meafures lefs violent, which in all probability will deter the criminal from his purpofe, though they do not proceed to the extent of difabling him.

No man has a right to inflict an additional punifhment, or any punifhment, upon an aggreffor, for the mere purpofe of deterring others from harbouring injurious intentions. The affertion of fuch a right would be directly repugnant to the principles of natural juftice eftablifhed in the third chapter. Yet if two juftifiable modes of punifhment fuggeft themfelves to the mind of the perfon injured, either

of

of which would anfwer his purpofe, he is bound in the fight of God to adopt that mode which appears moft likely to deter others from engaging in criminal undertakings. Inftead of punifhing the offender with ftripes, let him bind him to a tree by the way-fide, characterifed by fymbols of his guilt, if he thinks that the dread of fimilar difgrace will more ftrongly imprefs the traveller with abhorrence of the crime than the apprehenfion of corporal chaftifement.

The idea of inflicting punifhment by way of indemnification, or in lieu of it, is too abfurd to merit much attention. Punifhment, as fuch, can never conftitute indemnification; inflicted with this view it muft be nugatory; it would therefore be an unauthorifed violation of the rights of another.

Since the right of punifhment appears originally to be merely a branch of the right of defence againft an aggreffor, it follows, from what was proved in the difcuffion of this right, that it may be exercifed, if neceffary, by any individual, on behalf of another againft whom an unjuft attack is intended, whenever the
affiftance

assistance of the former is naturally due to the latter, or desired by him; and whenever the former apprehends that the defence of the latter is necessary for his own present or future security. It is also the duty of every man in the sight of God to exert the right of punishment, or to forbear from exercising it, in any particular instance, according as he is persuaded that such exertion or forbearance will most effectually promote the great purposes of his being. And in forming his judgment on these points, as well as in determining the mode of punishment to be adopted, it is his duty to consult the ends for which the aggressor was created, as far as is consistent with the other considerations, which he is to take into the account.

CHAP. VIII.

ON SLAVERY.

By flavery I mean the condition of a perfon who is compelled to labour at the will of another, without any previous contract.

Agreeably to natural juftice, an individual may be reduced by force to this condition on two accounts:

1ft: For Indemnification.

2dly: For Punifhment.

The caufes which may entitle one man to force another into flavery, for the fake of indemnification or punifhment, and the circumftances which fhould determine him to exert or to wave his right, have already been difcuffed in the two preceding chapters. The flavery, in thefe cafes, muft ceafe, as foon as the juft purpofes for which it was impofed are obtained. Until thefe are accomplifhed, the right of the impofer remains unaltered; and the exercife of it, during the whole or any part of its continuance, may be transferred by him to any other perfon.

He, who has taken his enemy captive in a conflict, has no right on that account to doom him to flavery. It is idle to fay that he might take the life of his conquered antagonift, and is therefore merciful in exacting only his labour. Let him eftablifh the premifes before he deduces the conclufion. All that he can claim from his captive is reparation for paft injuries, and fecurity againft future violence. If it be neceffary for the attainment of either of thefe ends that the latter fhould be enflaved, he may then, and then only, be enflaved confiftently with juftice.

In no cafe has the mafter a right to the labour of the guiltlefs family of the flave, further than the flave is himfelf entitled to exact it. Whatever right the flave may poffefs to the fervices of his children is liable, like any other of his rights, to be claimed and exercifed by the mafter, as far as he finds
that

that measure necessary for securing the just purposes of punishment and indemnification; but the right of the master over each child terminates as soon as that child attains to such an age as no longer to be subjected by nature to the dominion of his parent.

This reasoning applies with equal force to children born during the slavery of their parents. The master cannot derive from the latter more extensive or more permanent rights than they themselves possess over their offspring.

If the master, shifting the ground of argument, pleads that he has maintained the child from infancy to manhood, and not from gratuitous charity, but with a view to his own advantage; let him be reminded, that he has received in return the labour of the other during that period. But he replies, that " the
" labour has been an inadequate return; and
" that he has at least a right to exact the ser-
" vices of the child when grown up, until he
" has obtained a reasonable indemnification;
" for the infant having no prospect of being
" supported by any other person, it must be
" presumed that, had he been able, he would
" gladly

"gladly have consented to secure a mainte-
"nance on the terms of making an equitable
"compensation when he should have it in his
"power.' Why does not the master assert, that the other, had he been able, would have consented to secure his existence on *any* terms, and claim a right to detain him in *perpetual* bondage? Why does he not affirm that he has a right to enslave any man whom he has saved from drowning? No consent was or could be given in either case, nor any right conveyed. Whatever debt of gratitude may have been incurred, that is not to be recovered by compulsion. In each of these instances one of the most indispensable duties, which a human being can owe to his Maker, has been performed; and, although the performance should meet with no return in this world, yet, if it arose from proper motives, it will not pass without a final reward.

CHAP. IX.

ON PROPERTY.

It has already been proved that every man has originally a right, by the gift of God, to such a portion of the unappropriated productions of the earth as is necessary for his comfortable subsistence.

The first and most obvious exercise of this right would be the acquisition of food, of shelter, and of clothing. To this would succeed the fabrication of rude utensils and weapons.

The right however extends beyond the bare productions of the soil. The earth itself, together with its productions, forms one common stock for the benefit of mankind, any unappropriated part of which may be seized by each individual for his own exclusive possession, so long as that exclusive possession is requisite for his comfortable subsistence. The same wants,

wants, which, in confequence of being an evidence of the will of God, convey to any one a title to a certain portion of the fruits of the earth, in like manner give him a title to a certain portion of the earth itfelf. He has the fame inconteftable right to the unmolefted enjoyment of the fpot of ground, which he has covered with his tent, with his grain, or with his flocks, as he has to the fpot on which he is ftanding, or to that on which he lies afleep.

He, therefore, who, in confequence of thefe wants, has taken poffeffion of a vacant cavern for his habitation, and the adjoining unoccupied hill for the pafturage of his cattle, has authority from God to defend them againft every aggreffor. But the right which neceffity creates neceffity limits. He has no claim to a greater extent of land than is requifite for the comfortable fubfiftence of himfelf, and of the family, the flocks and herds, which God has given to him. If a favage, before America was inhabited, had been driven in his canoe from Tartary to Cape Horn, he would have had an indubitable right to the exclufive poffeffion of fuch a diftrict round his hut as was necessary

necessary for his support; but he would have had no right to object to future strangers settling on a distant part of the coast, on the plea that he stood in need of the whole continent for his hunting ground.

The cavern however, and the hill, the flocks, and the utensils, and whatever other articles of property had not been previously transferred by gift to some other, and become his actual right, must revert, on the dereliction or death of the owner, to the common stock, and be open to the next occupant. The former possessor's right was founded on his need, and extended only to the use of them; this need and this use cannot be prolonged beyond the term of his life; and he cannot convey a right to another, either by will or in any other method, beyond the period when that right necessarily terminates.

Mr. Paley and other moralists contend that those moveables, which are the produce of a man's personal labour, as his tools, weapons, &c. may originally be disposed of by will, because the owner has employed his own labour

labour upon them[a], and has inseparably mixed it with them[b], thereby giving them a great increase of value, which increase is inseparable from and makes a great part of the whole value.

The foregoing reasoning, notwithstanding the respectable names by which it is sanctioned, appears to rest on unsubstantial foundations. No man can prove any just title originally to appropriate to himself, either flocks, herds, and fruits, or any productions of the earth (as the materials whereof his weapons, utensils, and other moveables, may be formed), nor consequently to retain them afterwards, whatever alteration he may have wrought in them by his labour, except the right which arises from their being necessary for his comfortable subsistence; a right which is inevitably extinguished by his death.

If the arguments, by which Mr. Paley maintains that an individual has a natural right to dispose of his moveables by will, possessed any real force, they would prove him to have the same right to bequeath land, which he has reclaimed from barrenness to fertility. And,

[a] Paley, Vol. I. P. 221.   [b] Vol. I. P. 115, 116.

in fact, Mr. Paley maintains that land [c] under these circumstances becomes the property of the cultivator as absolutely as the utensils are which he has manufactured. He adds, that the individual, who thus improves it, does not thereby acquire a right to it in perpetuity, and after this cultivation and all its effects are ceased. It follows however, according to his statement, that the improver may by will convey to another a right over it for the period during which the effects of his labour shall continue. Yet in a subsequent [d] chapter he proceeds

[c] Vol. I. P. 116.

[d] P. 222.—Mr. Paley argues on this subject nearly in the manner which I have adopted—that " in a state of " nature a man's right to a particular spot of ground arises " from his using it and wanting it, consequently ceases " with the use and want; so that at his death the estate " reverts to the community, without any regard to the " last owner's will." Yet these are arguments to which Mr. Paley can give no weight consistently with his fundamental principle. He ought to have confined his researches to the single point, whether the existence of the power of bequeathing land in a state of nature would, or would not, promote the happiness of mankind. If this question be determined in the affirmative, he must maintain the existence of the right, in defiance of the arguments on which he has disproved it.

It is to be observed that, in asserting the right of bequeathing proceeds to establish the opposite conclusion, and to establish it on principles which admit of no exception, that land previous to the institution of civil society cannot be disposed of by testamentary bequest.

The principles which have been deduced in the present treatise oblige me to deny the existence of a right, which Mr. Paley, in common with other moralists, has supported; I mean the right of extreme necessity. This he defines to be ᵃ " a right to use or destroy " another's property, when it is necessary for " our own preservation to do so." And as an instance of it he mentions " a right to " take, without or against the owner's leave, " the first food, clothes, or shelter, we meet " with, when we are in danger of perishing " through want of them." And he asserts it to be " a general right, as it is incidental

queathing moveables, Mr. Paley pays no more attention to general expediency than he has done in disproving the right of bequeathing lands. The reader, who has perused his work attentively, will have perceived that it is not uncommon with him totally to lose fight of his fundamental principle, and to argue on other and less fallacious grounds.

ᵃ Page 102.

to

" to every man who is in a situation to
" claim it."

In the first place, I must observe that Mr. Paley has adduced no arguments to prove the only fact, which, according to his fundamental position, can demonstrate the existence of the right; namely, that arming every man with authority to deprive another of his property, whenever he imagines that property to be necessary for his preservation, would promote the happiness of mankind. How would it appear, were we to argue on his own principle of expediency, that this is a case " in which " the particular consequence exceeds the ge- " neral consequence," and that " the [f] remote " mischief resulting from the violation of the " general rule is overbalanced by the imme- " diate advantage?"

In the next place, I may be allowed to ask for the preservation of *what* particular objects may this right be exercised? Not merely of

[f] I have already quoted Mr. Paley's preliminary observation, that, " in computing consequences, it makes no dif- " ference in what manner or *at what distance* they ensue."

life, but of property also; for Mr. Paley authorises every man on *this* principle [*] to pull down a neighbour's house against his consent, to stop the progress of a fire: for the security then of what kinds of property may it not be exercised? Much more may not any man exercise it for the security of what is dearer than property, his health; of what is dearer than life, his good name? May not he forcibly possess himself of the house of another, should he be persuaded that his desire for it, if it be not gratified, will bring upon him death, or delirium, or melancholy? May he not seize his neighbour's purse, that he may be enabled to silence a venal calumniator, who threatens to ruin his character? In short, if the principle be admitted in any one instance, where is the line to be drawn?

" The foundation of the right," Mr. Paley says, " seems to be this; that, when property " was first instituted, the institution was not " *intended* to operate to the destruction of any; " therefore, when such consequences would " follow, all regard to it is superseded." The insufficiency of this mode of reasoning will appear

[*] Page 102.

pear by an application of it to other inftances. The right to defend ourfelves, with which we are endowed, was not *intended* to operate to the deftruction of any. Is it therefore never to be permitted fo to operate? The inftitution of municipal laws was intended for the *benefit* of every member of the fociety, and not for the deftruction of any; when therefore fuch confequences would follow, is all regard to it fuperfeded?

That no fuch right as that of extreme neceffity can exift has already been fhewn. It has been proved, in the difcuffion of the third propofition, that no man has a right to deprive another of his property, or to reftrain him in the enjoyment of it, without his confent having been previoufly given, unlefs the latter has invaded, or fhewn a defign to invade, the rights of the former, or of fome perfon under his protection.

The pofitions which have been maintained in this chapter, and in the three preceding chapters on Indemnification, Punifhment, and Slavery, are ftrictly applicable to the proceedings between independent ftates. The various modifications which thefe rules undergo, when applied to proceedings between members of the fame community, arife from the peculiar rights and obligations of governors and fubjects, which will be briefly inveftigated in a fubfequent chapter of this treatife.

CHAP. X.

ON ENGAGEMENTS.

A PROMISE is not a mere declaration of an intention; it is an engagement to the promisee that the promiser will act in the manner specified.

Consent understood to be given and accepted constitutes a promise; but less than this will not constitute one. If the promisee refuse to accept the right which the other offers to him, matters remain as they were before the offer was made.' Promises then do not exist before acceptance, and consequently are not binding.

The obligation to perform a promise, or any other engagement, is a branch of the general obligation not to infringe without just cause the rights of another. When an individual by any engagement has transferred to his neighbour one of the gifts which God has bestowed

bestowed upon him, the latter has the same right to it which the original proprietor had before the transfer; and if it be withheld from him he has the same right to use force for the recovery of it as for the recovery of any other article of his property. This reasoning is equally valid, whatever be the subject of the engagement.

If a traveller ask a shepherd the road to the place whither he is journeying, the latter is not originally under any obligation to the inquirer (whatever may be his duty in the sight of God) to communicate information. His knowledge is his own, and he may impart or withhold it at his discretion. The traveller requests him to impart it. If the shepherd returns such an answer as he knows the former will consider as an assent to his request, that is, as a direct or implied promise that he shall be put in possession of the knowledge in question, this knowledge is now become the actual property of the traveller; and he has the same right to use force, if force be necessary, for the purpose of obtaining it from the other, as he would have to obtain the delivery of a lamb which the shepherd had promised

to

to him, or the reſtitution of a horſe of which he had robbed him. The foregoing reaſoning is not affected by the manner in which an engagement is contracted. The obligation to performance reſts on every perſon who has contracted an engagement, whether it were expreſſed or implied, whether entered into by words or actions.

The ſhepherd might enter into an implied engagement to give the traveller right directions by wilfully directing him wrong; for he would know that the traveller would underſtand *any* directions not palpably abſurd as an aſſent to his requeſt. He might convey a promiſe by a nod as intelligibly as by the moſt poſitive aſſurances.

But the promiſer is not bound to thoſe to whom he could not be ſuppoſed to mean to engage himſelf. The ſtrongeſt aſſurances given to the traveller would not lay the ſhepherd under any obligation of ſhewing the road to a liſtener, whom he did not know to be at hand, or did not mean to addreſs.

" Where

" Where the terms of a promise admit of
" more senses than one, the promise is to be
" performed in that sense in which the pro-
" miser apprehended at the time that the
" promisee received it."

This [a] is Mr. Paley's rule for the interpretation of promises; and it is very just. He proves it in the following manner.

" It is not the sense, in which the promiser
" actually intended it, that always governs the
" interpretation of an equivocal promise; be-
" cause at that rate you might excite expect-
" ations which you never meant, nor would
" be obliged, to satisfy. Much less is it the
" sense in which the promisee actually
" received the promise; for according to that
" rule you might be drawn into engagements
" which you never designed to undertake.
" It must therefore be the sense (for there is
" no other remaining) in which the promiser
" believed that the promisee accepted his
" promise."

* Paley, Vol. I. P. 125.

For

For the satisfaction of any reader who may wish for a demonstration of the truth of the rule from first principles, the following is subjoined.

Consent, understood to be expressed by one party and to be accepted by the other, constitutes a promise. The promiser, therefore, is bound to fulfil what he meant to express and believed to be accepted; and the promisee has a right to claim what he meant to accept and believed to be expressed. If either of them apprehended that the other party had a different meaning from himself, but did not intimate his doubts and come to an explanation, he is bound to adhere to that different meaning; for by his silence he implied acquiescence in it. So that, in fact, the promiser is bound to fulfil what he believed to be accepted, and the promisee to claim no more than he believed to be expressed.

In certain cases promises are not binding.

1st: Where the promiser or the promisee is not a moral agent.

For under thofe circumftances the one cannot convey, nor the other acquire, any right.

Thus the promifes of infants, idiots, and lunatics, are naturally void.

So are the promifes of a drunken man, if at the time of making them he was fo far overpowered by intoxication as to be no longer a moral agent; but not otherwife. Whether he was a moral agent or not, muft be determined from particular facts; in the fame manner as you would afcertain the degree of mental diforder which conftitutes madnefs.

Perhaps it may be faid, that the drunken man, although not a moral agent, is anfwerable notwithftanding for his actions in that ftate; having reduced himfelf to it by his own voluntary act. That argument, if it had any force, would apply equally to the cafes of fuch idiots and lunatics as have brought their incapacity on themfelves by their own mifconduct; by the gratification of intemperance, or through the excefs of paffion. It is not, however, applicable in any of thefe cafes.

Although

Although every man who deprives himself of reason is answerable to God, yet if he be in fact, through whatever cause, no longer a moral agent, he is unable to convey any right; and what he cannot convey, the promisee cannot acquire from his consent.

In the preceding instances the promiser has been supposed not a moral agent; the rule would have appeared equally applicable had the promisee been represented in that situation.

2dly: Promises are not binding, when an express or implied condition, on which they are understood by both parties to be founded, fails without the fault of the promiser.

For the terms are not fulfilled on which alone the promise was to have existence.

Thus if a person undertakes to assist another, avowedly supposing him to be unjustly attacked, he is released from his promise, if he discovers the promisee to be the aggressor.

In contracts, which are mutual promises, if one party fails in the performance of his engagement,

engagement, the other is released; unless there was some previous stipulation to the contrary.

If the promiser be previously apprised of the failure of the condition, or wilfully occasion it, he violates his engagement, and may be compelled to make satisfaction.

These rules will be illustrated by a consideration of the case of promises, the performance of which is impossible.

Such promises are evidently not binding; for the possibility of performance is the only supposition on which the promise could be understood or accepted; and of course was a condition of the promise.

But if the promiser was privately aware of the impossibility when he made the promise; as if he engaged to put a tenant into immediate possession of a farm which he knew was under lease to another; or if he afterwards occasioned it, as by causing his daughter, after he had promised her in marriage to one person, to be united to a different man; the promisee has

has a right to compensation for the loss which he sustains by the non-performance: for in each case he acquired a right to the thing promised, and in each case the disappointment of his just claim, and the consequent injury which he receives, is owing to the wilful fault of the promiser.

3dly: Promises are not binding, the performance of which would be unjust, that is, would be an unauthorised infringement of the rights of a third person,

For the promiser cannot convey a right which is not his to dispose of; and consequently the promisee cannot acquire it.

If both parties were aware of the injustice of performance at the time when they entered into the engagement, the case is clear; neither of them can have a doubt of the promise being void; nor is the promiser bound to indemnify the other, as a right could never be supposed to be conveyed to him.

If both parties were, as far as appears, unapprised, at the time of engaging, of any
injustice

injuſtice attending the performance, the promiſee, on this injuſtice being diſcovered, (whether it did or did not exiſt when the promiſe was made) has no claim to indemnification: for all engagements, where nothing appears to the contrary, muſt be underſtood to have proceeded on the ſuppoſition, that is, on the implied condition, of the performance being compatible with juſtice.

But if the promiſer has wilfully occaſioned the injuſtice of performance; or if he was privately aware of it at the time of making the engagement, and the promiſee was ignorant of it; in either caſe he is liable to a juſt demand of compenſation: for by his promiſe he engaged to put the other party in poſſeſſion of the matter in queſtion, and is bound to make reparation for the diſappointment and injury which he has wilfully occaſioned.

The reaſoning which has been ſtated on the ſubject of promiſes, the performance of which is unjuſt, fully applies to promiſes which contradict a former valid engagement. For the right pretended to be conveyed by the

ſubſequent

subsequent promise was already transferred to another person by the former.

Mr. Paley [b] affirms, that the performance of a promise is unlawful, when it would be inconsistent with what he terms an *imperfect* obligation. It would not be a difficult undertaking to prove this rule to be erroneous in its principle [c]; and to shew that it has led, and must lead Mr. Paley, to conclusions the reverse of those which he has maintained on other grounds: but as the difference between the kinds of obligations which moralists have denominated perfect and imperfect, has not yet been specifically discussed in the present treatise, (nor would this be a fit place for the discussion) I shall only observe that, if the rule were true, no reliance could be placed on any engagement. The promiser would very

[b] Page 132.

[c] See particularly the instance of promising a person your vote (p. 132), which Mr. Paley adduces as an example of an imperfect obligation; and compare it with his observations on the same instance, p. 138. How can these decisions be reconciled, since Mr. Paley admits, p. 92, that you are always under an imperfect obligation to give your vote to the better candidate?

frequently discover some imperfect obligation, which would be violated by the performance; and in every case he would be able to feign such a discovery, without being liable to confutation.

I apprehend that other errors have been admitted into Mr. Paley's chapters on promises, and on lies, important enough to merit particular notice.

Mr. Paley affirms [d] that "a promise cannot be deemed unlawful, where it produces when performed no effect beyond what would have taken place had the promise never been made."

As he [e] advances no argument in support of this rule (and surely it is not self-evident), it

---

[d] Page 134.

[e] Perhaps Mr. Paley argued in his own mind that such a promise is lawful, because the performance occasions no injury to any one which would not otherwise have taken place; and therefore is not repugnant to general expediency. The topic of general expediency has been fully considered in the preceding pages.

it will be sufficient to prove it erroneous by an example. An assassin determines to kill a certain individual; he is afterwards defired by another to murder the same man, and engages to do it: according to the foregoing rule his promise is lawful, for he would have committed the murder if he had not made it. Or, let us suppose an instance somewhat less atrocious. A tyrant issues orders for the execution of an unconvicted prisoner, whose only crime has been a determined support of the liberties of his country: by Mr. Paley's rule, if a person ever so conscious of the innocence of the sufferer were to undertake to become the executioner of the usurper's vengeance, his engagement would be lawful. But are not these conclusions as repugnant to Mr. Paley's

The rule not being just, Mr. Paley's subsequent reasoning deduced from it, that " in this case the obligation of a " promise will justify a conduct, which unless it had been " promised would be unjust," falls to the ground. In no case will a promise bind any one to be guilty of a breach of justice, or vindicate the action.

The right of the captive, in Mr. Paley's instance, to regain his freedom by a promise of neutrality, arises from these circumstances; that the laws of nature and of his country leave him at liberty to enter into such an engagement if he thinks fit.

previous reasoning on unlawful promises, as they are to the principles which have been maintained in my present chapter?

Mr. Paley also affirms [f] that "falsehoods are not lies, that is, are not criminal, where the [g] person to whom you speak has no right to know the truth; or, more properly, when little or no inconvenience results from the want of confidence."

Both these rules appear to me destitute of any solid foundation.

In reply to the first it may be remarked, that if the person who has no right to know the truth is a moral agent, and you answer him in such a way as you think will lead him to conclude that you mean to impart to him the desired information, you *give* him a right to it; and you are guilty of a breach of promise, that is (according to Mr. Paley's definition) of a lie, if you do not communicate it: for, to proceed in his own words, "who-

---

[f] Page 184.   [g] Page 185.

"ever

"ever [h] seriously addresses his discourse to another, tacitly promises to speak the truth, because he knows that the truth is expected."

The second rule would authorise every man to lie at his own discretion. It is founded on general expediency, a principle which has been already refuted[i].

The practice of deceiving an enemy by feints, false colours, spies, and false intelligence, is justified according to Mr. Paley by the preceding rule. Without entering into particulars it may be observed, that the only stratagems which can be employed against an enemy, consistently with natural justice, are such as do not involve an express or implied promise of sincerity.

Extorted promises are binding.

[h] "A lie is a breach of promise." Paley, Vol. I. Page 184.

[i] Mr. Paley's decision under this rule, that you may tell a lie to a robber or an assassin to save your property or your life, cannot easily be reconciled with his doubts, p. 140, whether a promise extorted by them is binding.

This

[124]

This point has long been contested among moralists. To argue it fairly, we must suppose that the extorted promises are not such as would be void, if they were voluntary.

On what plea then is an exemption from the general obligation of performance claimed for him whose engagement was extorted?

1st: It is claimed, because the promiser entered into the engagement in consequence of violent constraint and apprehension.

By our previous supposition the promiser was a moral agent, capable of choosing and adopting either of the alternatives offered to him. How then did the force and apprehension affect him? They laid a strong bias on his will, and set before him a powerful temptation to make the promise. And does this render the promise void? If you affirm that it does, you must affirm the same in every case in which the promiser is under an inducement equally strong, arising from persuasion, or from interest, or from passion; for, provided the bias be laid on his will, and the temptation be set before him, it is of no more

consequence

consequence to the argument by what means this is effected, than it is whether the assailant in the present case attacked him with a sword or a club. And, since it is impossible to assign a reason why any particular degree of bias is the lowest which exempts a moral agent from the obligation of performance, you must ultimately maintain that every promise, contracted in consequence of any the most trifling inducement, is void; in other words, you must maintain that no man ever was bound, or ever will be bound, to perform any promise whatever.

2d: But the promiser, it is contended, notwithstanding his outward actions, did not give his mental consent. His mental reservations, which did not appear, were as immaterial to the validity of the promise as if they had never existed. He knew that every thing was done which constitutes a promise[k]; he

[k] Dr. Ferguson (Institutes of Moral Philosophy, 2d ed. p. 189.) contends, that an extorted promise is not binding, because the promisee could not have a reasonable expectation of its performance being intended. Surely he did expect it to be performed, or why was he at the trouble of

he knew that his consent was understood to be given, and that it was accepted by the other party. On the present plea, any voluntary engagement might be evaded, and any gift reclaimed. The promise under consideration was substantially made; why is it not faithfully performed?

3d: The promiser, it is finally asserted, is exempted from the obligation of performance by the principles which have been established in the preceding chapters: for it has there been proved, that every man has authority from God to attack any of the rights of an aggressor as far as self-defence requires. The promiser therefore, even if he admits the other party to have acquired a right through his engagement, may deprive him of this right, by withholding from the first the thing promised, or by forcibly reclaiming it if delivered; either the former [1] step being requisite for his

of exacting it? Whether his expectations were reasonable or not, is a matter of no consequence; since they were known to the other party, who by his promise engaged to satisfy them.

[1] Dr. Ferguson (p. 189, 2d edit.) alleges an argument of this kind.

self-defence,

self-defence, or the latter for his indemnification.

To this reasoning, which at first sight appears plausible, the following answer may be returned.

The promiser, it is granted, may attack, if necessity requires, any of the rights of the aggressor in self-defence; that is, in defence of any thing which is his own actual right at the time. But the thing which he has promised is no longer his right; he has made it the right of the promisee by his own transfer: previous to that transfer he might withhold it if demanded, or reclaim it if taken from him; but afterwards he has no more title to it than he has to any article of property belonging to any other person; and consequently has no pretence for detaining it on the plea of self-defence, nor for resuming it on the ground of indemnification [m].

[m] I am aware that I shall incur the charge of disorderly arrangement, by subjoining, to an inquiry into the nature of engagements in general, observations relating to a particular engagement, instituted in a particular country. Yet, as it is undeniably of great importance that just sentiments

ments should be entertained respecting the meaning of subscription to the thirty-nine articles, and as the opinion which Mr. Paley maintains on the subject appears to me not only unsupported by argument but likely to be productive of consequences highly pernicious, I trust the reader will pardon this deviation from the strictness of method.

Mr. Paley, having previously observed that the " animus " imponentis" indicates the sense in which the articles are to be subscribed, affirms, p. 219, that " the legislature of " the 13th Eliz. is the imposer."

The latter remark seems fundamentally erroneous.

The *present* legislature of this country, which by forbearing to exercise its acknowledged power of repealing the act of 13th Eliz. sanctions and enforces that act, is the imposer of subscription on the existing generation; and it is consequently the intention of the present legislature which the subscriber is bound to satisfy.

That subscription may be justified without an actual belief of each of the articles, as I understand Mr. Paley afterwards to intimate, is a gratuitous assumption. On this point the articles speak for themselves: Why is an article continued in its place if it be not meant to be believed? If one may be signed without being believed, why may not all? By what criterion are we to distinguish those which may be subscribed by a person who thinks them false, from those which may not? Is not the present mode of subscription virtually the same as if each article were separately offered to the subscriber? And in that case could any man be justified in subscribing one which he disbelieved?

No circumstance could have a more direct tendency to ensnare the consciences of the clergy, no circumstance could

could afford the enemies of the eftablifhed church a more advantageous occafion of charging her minifters with infincerity, than the admiffion of the opinion that the articles may fafely be fubfcribed without a conviction of their truth, taken feverally as well as collectively. That opinion I have feen maintained in publications of inferior note; but I could not without particular furprife and concern behold it avowed by a writer of fuch authority as Mr. Paley.

If the terms, in which any of the articles are expreffed, may be fairly interpreted in more fenfes than one; and if it be a known fact, that the generality of fubfcribers concur in one particular interpretation; that interpretation, efpecially if it has for fome time been ufually received, may be deemed to be one of the fenfes, if not the exclufive fenfe, in which affent is required by the legiflature; for, if it were not, the legiflature, it may be prefumed, would have altered the articles, or pointed out the precife meaning in which it defigned them to be underftood.

CHAP. XI.

GENERAL REVIEW OF THE NATURAL RIGHTS AND OBLIGATIONS OF MEN.

It has been ſtated heretofore, that by a right I mean authority from God for the enjoyment of any particular thing, or for the performance of any particular action.

It was alſo obſerved that the term right is occaſionally uſed, in compliance with cuſtom, to denote the object of a right; as when it is ſaid that life is one of the rights of man.

By natural rights are meant thoſe rights which an individual poſſeſſes independent of the inſtitution of civil ſociety.

Theſe rights, for the ſake of perſpicuity, I ſhall here enumerate, referring to the preceding chapters for particular information reſpecting each.

Every

Every individual naturally possesses

A right to life.

A right to freedom from personal injury and from personal restraint.

A right to appropriate to himself such a portion of the unappropriated productions of the earth, and such a portion of unappropriated land, as is necessary for his comfortable subsistence. The scriptures give him an equal right over animals.

A right to accept from others, and appropriate to himself, such rights as they have the power of transferring to him.

A right to defend any of his rights from an aggressor by the use of all requisite force against him; either by resisting his attacks, or by making the first attack upon him; or by imposing restraints and punishments on him; so far, and so far only, as is necessary for such defence.

A right, in cases of injury, to exact restitution, or indemnification, from the aggressor, by the use of all necessary force against him.

Lastly: A right to wave, to abridge, or to alienate, any of his rights at his own discretion; except such as he may himself have acquired under an express or implied condition to the contrary.

Right and obligation are correlative terms. Wherever any individual has a right, all others are under an obligation not to make an unjust attack upon it. In every such case they are under a special obligation both to God and the owner of the right; for God has a right to obedience, and the owner to freedom from injury. With respect to the exercise and disposal of his own rights, in such a manner as may best promote the purposes of his being, each individual is under an obligation to God alone.

No

No circumstance has more materially contributed to introduce confusion into moral reasoning than the various and even hostile significations of the word right. Not in conversation only; but, in books of repute, expressions like the following are common—
"It is right that you should relieve a
"beggar;"—"I have a right to refuse, if I
"think fit;"—"The Almighty has a right
"to your constant obedience;"—"I have a
"right to squander away my estate, though
"I know it will displease him." One principal source of these inconsistencies has been the injudicious practice of moralists, in dividing rights into two kinds, which they have termed perfect and imperfect. This division I have rejected on account of its radical inaccuracy. Under the title perfect, all rights whatever were in fact comprehended. Those denominated imperfect, were not rights, according to any consistent definition of that term. If I were told by a moral philosopher that a person in distress had a right to my charity, I should admit that he might have good reasons for presuming that I should relieve him; because he might reasonably expect that I should cheerfully employ the gifts

gifts which God had bestowed upon me, in a manner so conformable to the will of the donor; but I should deny that he had a *right* to that assistance from me which my Creator, when he constituted me a moral agent, gave me power to confer or to withhold at my discretion; a power, for the due exercise of which I am answerable to him alone.

The same argument would apply with equal force to all other *reasonable expectations*, which have been erroneously termed imperfect rights.

The introduction of imperfect rights was necessarily followed by a train of imperfect obligations. These rest on the same unsubstantial foundation with the supposed rights to which they correspond. Thus, I am under no obligation to a beggar to relieve him, because he has no right to my assistance. I am under an obligation to God to relieve the other, if I think upon the whole that it is the divine will that I should; because God has a right to my obedience. But this is a point which I am to decide for myself; and, in making the decision, it is my own conscience alone,

alone, and not the beggar's expectations, which I am bound to satisfy.

Mr. Paley adopts the division of rights and obligations into perfect and imperfect, though apparently against his better judgment.*— He also affirms, in conformity to his general principle, that " perfect rights can only be " distinguished by their value ᵇ." It should seem, according to this position, that a candidate at an election, who thinks the possession of the vacant seat as valuable to him as one of his estates, has as perfect a right to the former as he has to the latter. If this and other necessary consequences of the rule should be contradicted by some parts of Mr. Paley's work, that circumstance, far from obviating the arguments against the rule itself, will only shew at what opposite conclusions the most acute reasoner will arrive, who takes general expediency for his guide.

* Paley Vol. I. Page 91.   ᵇ Vol. II. Page 3.

PART III.

APPLICATION OF THE PRINCIPLES WHICH HAVE BEEN ESTABLISHED TO THE CONSTITUTION OF CIVIL SOCIETY.

CHAP. I.

THE TRUE GROUNDS OF CIVIL OBEDIENCE EXPLAINED.— ERRONEOUS NOTIONS REFUTED.

WHATEVER opinions may have been prevalent under the reign of the Stuarts, I apprehend that no intelligent Englishman, who shall have perused Mr. Paley's very satisfactory chapter " on the duty of Civil Obedi-
" ence as stated in the Christian Scriptures," will hesitate to admit that author's conclusion:
" That, as to the extent of our civil rights
" and obligations, Christianity hath left us
" where she found us; that she hath neither
" altered nor ascertained it; that the new
" Testament contains not one passage which,
" fairly interpreted, affords either argument
" or

" or objection applicable to any conclusions
" upon the subject, that are deduced from
" the law and religion of Nature."

This fundamental point being determined, I must recall the reader's attention to a proposition, the truth of which has already been proved: " That in no cases except the
" following is any person authorised to de-
" prive another of his natural rights, or to
" restrain him in the enjoyment of them."

1st: When he proceeds to such deprivation or restraint in consequence of immediate inspiration from God.

2ndly: Or in consequence of their being necessary for the defence of himself, or of some person under his protection, against the unauthorised attempts of another party.

3dly: Or in consequence of the consent of the individual thus deprived or restrained*.

* See Part II. Chap. III.

Since

Since there is no apparent probability that, in the prefent period of the world, infpiration will take place refpecting the circumftances, which form the fubject of this inquiry; and fince, if it fhould ever be proved to have taken place, the only line of conduct to be adopted would be implicit fubmiffion; the firft of the preceding cafes does not require further illuftration.

The force, exercifed in confequence of the neceffity ftated in the fecond cafe, is juftifiable only to the extent and during the continuance of that neceffity. Situations may poffibly arife in which, on the plea of this neceffity, an aggreffor may be compelled by his opponent to enter into civil fociety with him, or a conquered country to connect itfelf with the victorious ftate. Yet in fuch cafes the confent of the vanquifhed, though extorted, is the circumftance which lays them under the focial obligation; for it was in their option either to endure extremities, or to fubmit [b].

[b] All aggreffors are under an obligation to fubmit to fuch reftraints as the other party has a right to impofe in felf-defence. But this obligation is perfectly diftinct from that which refults from focial union.

Therefore

Therefore the only just foundation of civil government is the consent of the governed.

As this conclusion immediately and incontestably follows from principles, the validity of which has been established in the preceding pages, it cannot be necessary to enter into a prolix refutation of the various unsubstantial 1 eas on which governors, in different ages and different parts of the world, have rested their claim to dominion. Yet, on account of the importance of the subject, it may not be useless to return a short and distinct answer to such of those pleas as have been most commonly maintained in theory or in practice.

If the governor, like an Eastern monarch, rests his claim on the superior dignity of his own nature, and thence infers that he has a right to compel his fellow-creatures to obey, for the purpose of promoting either his happiness or their own; what reply shall we give to an argument, which, if it were solid, would authorise every man to enslave his less enlightened neighbour, and would justify a Newton in seizing the sovereignty of the world? We may recur to that train of reasoning,

reasoning, by which it has been already proved that no man would be authorised, on the plea of promoting the happiness either of himself or of another, even if the object could certainly be attained, forcibly to restrain an unoffending individual in the exercise of his natural lights.

Should assumed dominion be vindicated on the grounds of general expediency, the ground on which Mr. Paley founds every right of the civil governor, I shall only observe that, if this plea has not already been abundantly overthrown, I must despair of alleging any satisfactory argument on [c] the subject.

Perhaps the claim is rested on the ground of conquest or captivity. If the war was not undertaken by the victors either in the just defence of themselves, or of others under their protection, it was an unauthorised attack on their opponents; and success in such an attack gives the conqueror no right to restrain his vanquished or captive antagonist

[c] See Part II. Chap. III.

against

against his will. If the latter, presented only with a choice of evils, agrees to acknowledge the authority of his too fortunate enemy, the governor has then acquired a right to enforce submission; but he has acquired it from the consent of his subject. Until that consent is expressly or impliedly given, the pretended sovereign is an usurper; and has no better title to the fruits of his conquest than an highwayman has to his booty. If the war was originally just, the conqueror has a right to exercise dominion over the defeated party, so far as is necessary to ensure to himself indemnification for the injuries which he has sustained, and security from any further violence which he believes to be meditated. After the attainment of these purposes, consent alone can authorise the continuance of his jurisdiction, and invest him with civil authority.

But perhaps the governor grounds his claim to sovereignty on the single circumstance of the individual, whose obedience he requires, having been born within his territories. In this enlightened part of Europe he cannot
mean

mean to have the claim underſtood according to the exploded notions of feudal vaſſalage. He cannot mean to imply that man is attached, like a tree, to the ſpot of land on which he is originally placed; that he is an appendage inſeparable from the ſoil, and neceſſarily ſubject to the ſame reſtrictions. He muſt confeſs that God has beſtowed upon every man certain natural rights, in whatever region he may chance to paſs the firſt moments of his exiſtence; and muſt explain his claim to imply, that the conſtitution of the country entitles him to allegiance from every perſon born within the limits of its juriſdiction. How then has the individual in queſtion loſt his natural right to freedom? Has he forfeited it by his crimes? That is not pretended; the claim of allegiance embraces alike the innocent and the guilty.— In what manner therefore have the conſtitution and laws of the country acquired authority to control his original rights? Theſe rights, until he arrived at ſuch an age as to be juſtly deemed a moral agent, may have been at the difpoſal of his parents or protectors: when that period is arrived are they

not

not abſolutely his own by the gift of God? By the gift of God they are abſolutely his own; and, as long as he abſtains from invading the rights of others, no perſon whatever can claim any juriſdiction over him, until it be ſanctioned by his expreſs or implied conſent.

CHAP.

CHAP. II.

ORIGIN OF CIVIL GOVERNMENT.

"Government at firſt was either patriar-
"chal or military; that of a parent over his
"family, or of a commander over his fellow-
"warriors [a]."

Were I to undertake the defence and illuſ-
tration of this poſition ſtated by Mr. Paley, I
could not accompliſh my deſign in any method ſo effectual, as by tranſcribing his own
very accurate diſcuſſion of the ſubject. I will
not, by abridging his remarks, exhibit them
to diſadvantage; nor ſhould I dwell longer
on this topic, were it not for the purpoſe of
ſhewing that the rights of civil government
appear from Mr. Paley's account of their origin (however unfavourable to his own ſyſtem
that appearance may be) to have been eſta-
bliſhed on conſent alone.

[a] Paley, Vol. II. P. 111.

Having

Having alluded to the rights which parents naturally possess over their children, previously to their arrival at years of discretion, Mr. Paley observes, that " a parent [b] would retain " a considerable part of his authority after " his children were grown up, and had " formed families of their own. The obe-" dience, of which they remembered not " the beginning, would be considered as " natural; and would scarcely during the " parent's life be entirely or abruptly with-" drawn." These words imply that the children, when grown up, were at liberty to withdraw their obedience, had they thought proper to take this step. And this inference is confirmed by Mr. Paley's observations on the rights and duties of parents in another part of his work; wherein he proves that the former owe their origin and validity to the latter; and that the right of coercion exists no longer than it is necessary for the purpose of enabling the parent to ensure the welfare of his child, as yet too young to provide for himself. When therefore that period is elapsed, all further subjection on the part of the child must be voluntary.

[b] Page 112. Vol. II.

That the succeffor of the parent derives his authority folely from the confent of the other members of the fociety, Mr. Paley evidently allows; fince he defcribes him as "appointed to his office by their own " formal choice," or by a " willing transfer" of their obedience, encouraged perhaps by motives of refpect for their firft anceftor.

That the military chief owes his [d] appointment to the confent of his fellow-warriors is a fact fufficiently obvious.

Laftly: The caufes which Mr. Paley enumerates,[e] as having given rife to the rule of hereditary fucceffion, are all of them motives by which the members of a community would be induced to eftablifh that rule by confent; but they do not, either fingly or collectively, afford an argument to prove that by any other means than confent the eftablifhment could juftly have taken place.

[c] P. 113. [d] P. 114. [e] P. 115.

CHAP.

CHAP. III.

EXAMINATION OF SOME OF MR. PALEY'S OBJECTIONS TO THE ESTABLISHMENT OF CIVIL OBEDIENCE ON CONSENT.

THOUGH I apprehend it to have been clearly proved, that the confent of the fubject is the only juft foundation on which civil government can be eftablifhed; yet the authority of Mr. Paley, who totally rejects this doctrine, is fo great as to entitle his arguments to diftinct confideration. I fhall enter into an examination of them with greater willingnefs, as, in the courfe of it I fhall have an opportunity of making fome remarks, which may tend to elucidate the true nature of focial polity.

The theory againft which Mr. Paley immediately directs his attack, is a theory which I think by no means unobjectionable. I fhall proceed to feparate thofe parts of it which are indefenfible from thofe which appear to reft on immovable foundations; after premifing that

that it is not this theory alone, but every theory which grounds civil obedience on the confent of the fubject, that Mr. Paley labours to explode. He ᶠ rejects the intervention of a compact " as unfounded in its principle, and " dangerous in the application;" and fub- ftitutes ᵍ " public expediency in the place of all " implied compacts, promifes, and conven- " tions whatfoever."

Mr. Paley obferves that the compact, which Mr. Locke and other political writers affirm to fubfift between the citizen and the ftate, is twofold.

" Firft ʰ : An *exprefs* compact by the pri-
" mitive founders of the ftate, who are fup-
" pofed to have convened for the declared
" purpofe of fettling the terms of their poli-
" tical union, and a future conftitution of
" government : the whole body is fuppofed,
" in the firft place, to have unanimoufly con-
" fented to be bound by the refolutions of
" the majority; that majority, in the next
" place, to have fixed certain fundamental re-
" gulations; and then to have conftituted,

ᶠ Paley, Vol. II. P. 141.   ᵍ P. 143.   ʰ P. 130.

" either

" either in one perfon or in an affembly,
" (the rule of fucceffion or appointment be-
" ing at the fame time determined) *a ſtanding
" legiſlature*, to whom, under thefe pre-efta-
" bliſhed reſtrictions, the government of the
" ſtate was thenceforward committed; and
" whofe laws the feveral members of the
" convention were, by their firſt undertaking,
" thus perfonally engaged to obey. This
" tranfaction is fometimes called the *focial
" compact*; and thefe fuppofed original regu-
" lations compofe what are meant by the
" *conſtitution*, the *fundamental laws of the
" conſtitution*; and form on one fide the *in-
" herent indefeafable prerogative* of the crown,
" and on the other the *unalienable birth-
" right* of the fubject."

" Secondly: A *tacit* or *implied* compact, by
" all fucceeding members of the ſtate, who,
" by accepting its protection, confent to be
" bound by its laws; in like manner, as
" whoever *voluntarily enters* into a private
" fociety is underſtood, without any other
" or more explicit ſtipulation, to promife a
" conformity with the rules, and obedience
" to the government, of that fociety, as the
" known

" known conditions upon which he is ad-
" mitted to a participation of its privileges."

" This account of the subject, although
" specious, and patronised by names the most
" respectable, appears to labour under the
" following objections; that it is founded
" upon a supposition, false in fact, and leading
" to dangerous conclusions."

In support of these objections, Mr. Paley proceeds, in the first p ace, to contest the existence of the *express* compact stated and described above. He observes [1] that " no
" social compact, similar to what is here
" described, was ever made or entered into
" in reality; no such original convention of
" the people was ever actually held, or in
" any country could be held, antecedent to
" the existence of civil government in that
" country.

" It is to suppose it possible to call savages
" out of caves and deserts, to deliberate and
" vote upon topics, which the experience,
" and studies, and refinements, of civil life

[1] Page 132.

" alone

" alone suggest. Therefore no government
" in the universe began from this original."

Afterwards Mr. Paley adds, in reply to those who propose this original compact, not as a fact, but as a fiction, which furnishes a convenient explanation of the nature of civil government, that, " if [k] it be not a fact, it is " *nothing*; can confer no actual authority " upon laws or magistrates; nor afford any " foundation to rights, which are supposed " to be real and existing."

In this formidable attack on the existence and efficacy of Mr. Locke's *original* compact I entirely concur. I admit that no such compact ever did or could exist in any country; that no government in the world has been thus established; and that a supposed fictitious compact can never create a substantial right. But I must also remark, that the existence or non-existence of this original compact is a matter of perfect indifference to my argument; and a speculation wholly unimportant to the present members of any society. It

[k] Page 134.

has already been shewn, that every man capable of moral agency is originally poffeffed of various rights by the immediate gift of God; rights which no ftipulations of his anceftors can fhackle and abridge, nor any power juftly infringe againft the confent of the poffeffor, until he has forfeited them by his crimes. His birthright is not unalienable; but it is alienable only by himfelf. If therefore fuch an original compact had ever taken place, it would not have been obligatory on fucceeding generations. They in their turn would enjoy from their Maker's bounty the fame liberty with which their forefathers were endowed, of inftituting fuch a form of government as they fhould deem for their advantage; and of modelling, of curtailing, and of annihilating, whatever had been termed the inherent and inextinguifhable prerogative of the crown.

Mr. Paley, in the next place, points his artillery againft the *implied* compact. "[1] The "native fubjects of modern ftates are not "confcious of any ftipulations with their "fovereigns; of ever exercifing an election

---

[1] Page 136.

" whether

" whether they will be bound or not by the
" acts of the legiflature; of any alternative
" being propofed to their choice; of a pro-
" mife either required or given; nor do they
" apprehend that the validity or authority of
" the laws depends at all upon their recog-
" nition or confent. In all ftipulations,
" whether they be expreffed or implied,
" private or public, formal or conftructive,
" the parties ftipulating muft both poffefs
" the liberty of affent and refufal, and alfo
" be confcious of this liberty; which cannot
" with truth be affirmed of the fubjects of
" civil government, as government is now
" or ever[m] was adminiftered. This is a
" defect which no arguments can excufe or
" fupply; all prefumptions of confent, with-
" out this confcioufnefs, or in oppofition to
" it, are vain and erroneous."

If we fhould admit Mr. Paley's ftatements in this extract to be accurate in their utmoft latitude, they would fhew that government

[m] It is obvious that this affertion is incompatible with thofe parts of Mr. Paley's Chapter on the Origin of Civil Government which have been recently quoted and confidered.

has

has not *in fact* been established on the principle of the subject having given his consent; but they do not afford the shadow of an argument to prove that it can *justly* be established on any other principle: they contain not a single expression which may lead to prove a *right* in a civil governor to exact obedience, without having previously obtained the express or implied consent of the governed. I might therefore dismiss the objection, as totally irrelevant in an inquiry into the just foundation of civil government.

But these positions of Mr. Paley, if understood in that extent which the words seem naturally to imply, do not give an adequate representation of the case as it really exists. With respect to our own government in particular, the fact is in many instances the reverse of the preceding description. Not only our ablest political writers inculcate the doctrine of civil government originating from the consent of the governed; not only the public speakers in both houses of parliament, however numerous, and however essential the topics may be on which they differ, universally concur in vindicating the native right of the people to frame their own fyftem of government, and thereby at once manifeft and guide the general opinion of the nation; but almoft every fubject of the realm is apprized that the fovereign at his coronation binds himfelf by a folemn oath to obferve certain ftipulations, impofed on the part of of his fubjects to mark the limits of his power; and believes that the wilful violation of them would abfolve him from allegiance. This principle is fo well underftood by Englifhmen, and the fignal recognition of it at the period of the Revolution has received fuch general applaufe, that few, even if felected from the loweft and moft unenlightened claffes, would not think themfelves releafed on this very principle from the obligation of obedience (however neceffity might conftrain them to acquiefce,) if their monarch were to eftablifh the Roman catholic religion, or to transfer his dominions as a province to France. The preceding obfervations may be applied, in a greater or lefs degree, to moft, if not all, European governments.

It may alfo be obferved, with refpect to moft ftates in this part of the world, and particularly

larly concerning our own, that every man is confcious that if he continues in the dominions of the ftate he muft implicitly fubmit to its laws; and confequently by this continuance he tacitly and decidedly confents to obey them [n]. And his confent is accepted by the ftate through the medium of the laws, which defcribe what perfons fhall be confidered as fubjects. Whether he is aware of the contents of all, or of any, of thefe laws is a matter of no confequence. My reader confiders himfelf under a general obligation to fubmit to the prefent laws of the land, though perhaps there are few among them with which he is accurately acquainted.

But, it may be faid, numbers are little informed, or totally ignorant, refpecting thefe

[n] Mr. Paley, p. 137, ftates that the writers in favour of the implied compact maintain that allegiance is more efpecially promifed by the purchafe and inheritance of lands. As I have not refted any part of my argument on the circumftance of holding lands (although a circumftance affording an open proof of the occupier conforming to the laws and confenting to be a member of the ftate), it is not neceffary for me particularly to confider his remarks on that branch of the fubject.

original

original rights, and obey without confideration. And it muſt be owned that government is a ſyſtem too complex, and too far removed from the common apprehenſion of the crowd, to make it poſſible that in any ſtate it ſhould be univerſally underſtood. The intelligent alone will have a complete inſight into its principles and mechaniſm; others, as they gradually deſcend in the ſcale of ſociety, will entertain ideas more and more imperfect; until perhaps, in the very loweſt claſs, both knowledge and curioſity, with regard to the juſt grounds of ſubmiſſion, may be almoſt extinguiſhed. Nor is this partial ignorance peculiar to the ſubject of government; it prevails in a ſimilar degree, and with conſequences more to be lamented, with reſpect to religion. Yet neither in theſe, nor in any other examples, is any man diveſted of his native rights by the accidental circumſtance of having lived in ignorance of them; nor precluded from reclaiming, when he awakes from his trance, the liberty which he has received from heaven. The ſlave, who has neither ſurrendered his freedom by his conſent, nor forfeited it by his crimes, retains his title to it ſound and unimpaired, though

he

he may have toiled for half a century infenfible of the injuftice of his bondage; as the Indian preferves his claim to the bleffings purchafed for him by the death of Chrift, though he never heard of the name or of the exiftence of his Redeemer.

As, on the one hand, the fubject is not divefted of his natural rights by his ignorance of their exiftence, fo neither is the ftate deprived of its title to his obedience in confequence of his having confented to obey on erroneous grounds, provided it has not contributed to create or to prolong his blindnefs.

But " if the [*] fubject be bound only by his " own confent, and if the voluntary abiding " in a country be the proof and intimation of " that confent; by what arguments," demands Mr. Paley, " fhall we defend the right, which " fovereigns univerfally affume, of prohibit- " ing when they pleafe the departure of their " fubjects out of the realm?" I have advanced nothing which lays me under an obligation of defending every right affumed or exercifed by fovereigns. The pofition, which

[*] Page 137.

I have

I have undertaken to maintain, that the only juft foundation of civil government is the confent of the fubject, may be inconteftably true, although the practice mentioned by Mr. Paley fhould be utterly indefenfible. It may however be remarked, that if the ftate find it effentially requifite, for the purpofes of juftifiable felf-defence, to prohibit, either by a law enacted on the particular occafion, or by a difcretionary power vefted in the hands of a deputed legiflature, the departure of its fubjects out of the realm, left they fhould affift the enemy with intelligence, with their fubftance, or with their perfonal fervice, the impofition of this reftraint is an exercife of a juft right; and it is a reftraint which, under thofe circumftances, the ftate would be juftified in impofing on every inhabitant of the realm, whether citizen or foreigner. The prohibition, whenever it is not thus required by neceffity, cannot be vindicated. But, if juftifiable felf-defence require the general law, and its operation fhould accidentally detain a particular individual, who might fafely have been permitted to depart, the ftate, if it be unable to devife a teft whereby thofe perfons whofe departure would be compatible with

its

[160]

its security may be ascertained, is no more culpable than he who should unintentionally wound a harmless passenger by discharging a pistol at an assassin. It would be more obviously unreasonable to accuse the state of confining the subject, and exacting obedience without his consent, if poverty, or an accidental circumstance of a similar nature, should prevent him from leaving the country. If a tenant find himself compelled to hold a farm against his will, by being unable to bear the expense of removal, or in consequence of having broken his leg, the landlord is not chargeable with detaining him, nor does he forfeit his title to the rent.

" Still ᵠ less is it possible," adds Mr. Paley,
" to reconcile, with any idea of stipulation,
" the practice, in which all European nations
" agree, of founding allegiance upon the cir-
" cumstance of nativity; that is, of claiming
" and treating as subjects all those who are
" born within the confines of their dominions,
" although removed to another country in
" their youth or infancy. In this instance

ᵠ Page 136.

" certainly

" certainly the state does not presume a
" a compact."

I must again observe, that this practice, and other practices of states, may be diametrically opposite to the position, that just government can be established only on consent, and yet that position may be true. What is right is often the reverse of what is fact. Numberless actions arise daily from motives the most depraved; yet obedience to God is the only just principle of conduct. I will not repeat the reflections contained in the preceding chapter, on the obligation of allegiance being founded on the circumstance of birth. I cannot however refrain from remarking, that the practice of executing as rebels those who are taken in arms against the country in which they were born, although they have been nurtured in a foreign realm from their earliest infancy, is to be vindicated on no plea, except that of self-defence; and, without the strongest proofs of its being necessary for that purpose, cannot be rescued from the charge of barbarity and injustice.

M CHAP.

CHAP. IV.

MR. PALEY'S REMAINING OBJECTIONS CONSIDERED.
COMPARATIVE VIEW OF THE TWO SYSTEMS.

" THE [a] theory of government, which
" affirms the exiſtence and obligation of the
" ſocial compact, would, after all, merit little
" diſcuſſion; and, however groundleſs and
" unneceſſary, ſhould receive no oppoſition
" from us, did it not appear to lead to con-
" cluſions unfavourable to the improvement
" and to the peace of human ſociety."

This is an obſervation which very naturally
ſuggeſts itſelf to a moraliſt, who pronounces
on the rectitude of every action, and the
obligation of every duty, ſolely according to
his ideas of utility. Mr. Paley, in ſupport of
his allegations, urges three additional objections
to the doctrine of the rights of government
being founded on the conſent of the ſubject,
deſigned to ſhew the pernicious conſequences

[a] Page 138.

which would enfue from admitting it. Thefe objections I fhall diftinctly confider; but, previoufly to any examination of them, I muft obferve that, if the pofition, againft which their force is directed, has already been proved by found reafoning, not even a demonftration that its reception would be followed by undefirable effects would afford an argument againft its truth. The ravages of an eruption do not difprove the exiftence of the volcano.

Mr. Paley's firft objection is couched in the following terms; " Upon [b] the fuppofition
" that government was firft erected by, and
" that it derives all its juft authority from
" refolutions entered into by a convention of
" the people, it is capable of being prefumed
" that many points were fettled by that con-
" vention anterior to the eftablifhment of
" the fubfifting legiflature; and which the
" legiflature confequently has no right to alter
" or interfere with. Thefe points are called
" the *fundamentals* of the conftitution; and,
" as it is impoffible to determine how many
" or what they are, the fuggefting of any
" fuch ferves extremely to embarrafs the de-

[b] Page 138.

" liberations

" liberations of the legiflature, and affords a
" dangerous pretence for difputing the autho-
" rity of the laws."

Thefe arguments apply folely to the *original exprefs* compact afferted by Mr. Locke: I have already denied the exiftence of any fuch compact; and have further endeavoured to fhew, that, even if it had exifted, the prefent generation could not have been divefted of their natural rights by the ftipulations of their anceftors. I fhould not therefore have thought it neceffary to quote the preceding paragraph, had it not been for the purpofe of fubjoining this obvious remark. The bad confequences enumerated therein will not flow from the fuppofition that an individual, by voluntarily continuing in the ftate, *impliedly* confents to fubmit to the exifting laws, and thus confers on the community a title to his obedience.

Mr. Paley, in the fecond place, alleges that, " if 'it be by virtue of a compact that
" the fubject owes obedience to civil govern-
" ment, it will follow that he ought to abide
" by the form of government which he finds
" eftablifhed, be it ever fo abfurd or incon-

' Page 139.

" venient:

"venient: he is bound by his bargain. It is not permitted to any man to retreat from his engagement merely becaufe he finds the performance difadvantageous, or becaufe he has an opportunity of entering into a better. This law of contracts is univerfal."—"Refiftance to the *encroachments* of the fupreme magiftrate may be juftified upon this principle; recourfe to arms, for the purpofe of bringing about an amendment of the conftitution, never can."—"Defpotifm is the conftitution, of many ftates; and while a defpotic prince exacts from his fubjects the moft rigorous fervitude, according to this account, he is only holding them to their agreement."

I give Mr. Paley's arguments in his own words, that they may appear with their utmoft force: their validity refts wholly on a prefumption that it neceffarily follows, from the affertion of a compact, that, whenever an individual becomes a member of a community, he thereby engages to abide by the fyftem of government which he finds eftablifhed, as long as his governors fhall abftain from encroachments. But, until Mr. Paley's hypothefis thesis be substantiated, his objection can have no real weight.

When an individual enters into a civil society, his implied promise to obey the laws necessarily supposes that he is also admitted to enjoy the rights of a citizen. It is given, not, in the first instance, to the prince or legislative body, but to the state at large; and to the legislature only in virtue of its possessing the delegated authority of the state. The citizens of each community are the source and fountain of civil power, which, it has been proved, can be established on no just grounds except their consent; and their obligation to obedience is commensurate with the right which they have themselves created in the legislature, by a special grant of power, either express or implied. If therefore we admit, in the case of any particular government, that the legislature has not transgressed its appointed bounds; yet, unless it can be demonstrated that the citizens have at some particular period deprived themselves of their natural right of reclaiming at their discretion this deputed authority, by entering into an engagement that the grant shall be irrevocable;

and

and unlefs it can be further fhewn, that every fucceeding member of the ftate has alfo bound himfelf by the fame engagement; the whole of Mr. Paley's argument falls to the ground.

That thefe engagements do *neceſſarily* exift in every civil fociety is not furely to be prefumed as felf-evident.

There is, in truth, no better reafon for prefuming that he, who, by voluntarily becoming a member of a community, gives the legiflature a deputed power over him, does thereby engage never to refume the grant; than there would be for concluding that he, who takes a houfe at a certain rent, does thereby engage to hold it during his life on the fame terms; or that he, who voluntarily becomes the fervant of another, does thereby contract never to quit his place, or to infift on making a frefh bargain, as long as his mafter ufes him well, and pays him his prefent wages. Such engagements can never be fuppofed; they muft be proved by exprefs ftipulation.

"Every [d] violation of the compact on the part of the governor releases the subject from his allegiance, and dissolves the government. I do not perceive how we can avoid this consequence, if we found the duty of allegiance upon compact, and confess any analogy between the social compact and other contracts. In private contracts, the violation or non-performance of the conditions by one of the parties vacates the obligation of the other. Now the terms and articles of the social compact being no where extant or expressed; the rights and offices of the administrator of an empire being so many and various; the imaginary and controverted line of his prerogative being so liable to be overstepped in one part or other of it; the position that every such transgression amounts to a forfeiture of the government, and consequently authorises the people to withdraw their obedience, and provide for themselves by a new settlement, would endanger the stability of every political fabric in the world, and has, in fact, always supplied the disaffected with a topic of seditious

[d] Page 140.

"declamation.

" declamation. If occasions have arisen in
" which this plea has been resorted to with
" justice and success, they have been occa-
" sions in which a revolution was defensible
" on other and plainer principles: the plea
" itself is at all times captious and unsafe."

That every wilful violation of the compact on the part of government would authorise the people to withdraw their obedience, even if it were supposed that they had not the right independent of such violation, I admit; but that every such violation dissolves the government (as Mr. Paley asserts) is an inference which by no means necessarily follows, and an inference which is contradicted by the analogy of other contracts. If a private person appoints an agent, under certain stipulations, to manage his affairs for an unlimited time; and the latter, in a particular instance, should knowingly transgress the bounds of his power; it does not inevitably follow that his agency ceases from that moment. His employer, on being informed of his conduct, has a right to displace him; but, if he passes over in silence what has happened, the other continues in full possession of his office, and his future acts as agent are valid. This reasoning exactly applies to the situation of a governor and his subjects. He is their agent, with a prerogative by no means so indefinite as Mr. Paley seems to represent it, but determined by the known laws and usages of the land; and, although he may have exercised unconstitutional authority, yet he does not thereby cease at once to be governor. The people, it is true, may discharge him from his office; but if they are induced by prudential considerations, or by reflections on human weakness, to refrain from deposing him, he continues to have the same title to obedience from every member of the state as he had previously to the commission of the crime for which he might have been stripped of his power.

Mr. Paley proceeds to point out seven inferences, which he affirms to be important, and to " result * from the substitution of public " expediency in the place of all implied com- " pacts, promises, or conventions whatsoever." Without immediately entering into a professed inquiry how far the whole of these consequences in their full extent are beneficial, I

* Page 143.

shall

shall, in the first place, examine whether they are peculiar to Mr. Paley's system.

1st: " It may be as much a duty at one
" time to resist government as it is at an-
" other to obey it; to wit, whenever more
" advantage will, in our opinion, accrue to
" the community from resistance than mis-
" chief." The principle, on which I have endeavoured to establish the duty of submission, by no means excludes the duty of resistance. On that principle, subjects have a *right* to resist; not indeed, as Mr. Paley maintains, merely according to their ideas of expediency; but whenever the legislature exceeds the bounds of the authority with which it is intrusted, or persists in retaining that authority without possessing, either by stipulation or acquiescence, the consent of the community. And it is the *duty* of subjects to exert that right whenever they are persuaded that the purposes of their being, one of the most important of which is to promote the welfare of all orders of the state, will not be answered by forbearance as effectually as by resistance.

2dly:

2dly: "The lawfulnefs of refiftance, or the lawfulnefs of a revolt, does not depend alone upon the grievance which is fuftained or feared; but alfo upon the probable expenfe and event of the conteft."

This is the fecond of Mr. Paley's inferences, and together with it I fhall confider the fourth; as the fubftance of both is the fame, though clothed in different expreffions.

"Not every invafion of the fubjects rights, or liberties, or of the conftitution; not every breach of promife or of oath; not every ftretch of prerogative, abufe of power, or neglect of duty by the chief magiftrate, or by the whole or any branch of the legiflative body, juftifies refiftance; unlefs thefe crimes draw after them public confequences of fufficient magnitude to outweigh the evils of civil difturbance."

I muft requeft the reader to recollect the diftinction, which I have had frequent occafion to notice, between acts of duty to God and of juftice to men. The preceding quotations from Mr. Paley, confidered as referring only

only to actions of the former clafs, are perfectly compatible with the principle which I have afferted to be the only juft foundation of government, and are immediately deducible from the propofitions [f] eftablifhed in a former part of this treatife. The citizen who refifts an ufurper, or a tyrant, is guilty of a breach of duty towards God, if he refifts when forbearance would equally have enabled him to accomplifh the ends for which he was created; and I have already obferved, that to promote the happinefs of others is one of the moft important of thofe ends. They, who concerted the revolution, would not have been guilty of any injuftice towards James, even though they had oppofed him without having any profpect of fuccefs; but they would have flagrantly violated their duty to God, had they engaged in a hopelefs or unpromifing enterprize, which would neceffarily have produced the calamities of a civil war, and probably have riveted more ftrongly the fetters of their fellow fubjects.

[f] Part II. Chap. III. and IV.

3d: "Irregularity in the firſt foundation of a ſtate, or ſubſequent violence, fraud, or injuſtice in getting poſſeſſion of the ſupreme power, are not ſufficient reaſons for reſiſtance, after the government is once peaceably ſettled."

A peaceable ſettlement of the government proves that the ſubjects conſent to the ſovereignty of the prince on the throne, by whatever means he may have obtained poſſeſſion of it. And they have in all caſes a right to give this conſent, except it has been alienated or forfeited by their own act. The rule then is equally applicable, whether government be founded on conſent or on expediency.

4th: The fourth of Mr. Paley's inferences has already been conſidered.

5th: "No uſage, law, or authority whatever, is ſo binding, that it need or ought to be continued, when it may be changed with advantage to the community."

It

It has been sufficiently shewn in the preceding pages, that every law, whether it relate to the family of the prince, the order of succession, the form and authority of the legislature, or the duties of the subject, is mutable at the will of the community; except as far as the members of the state have abridged, by particular stipulations, their natural right of altering the laws.

The rule thus limited is an immediate consequence of the position, which establishes government on consent.

Mr. Paley proceeds to deduce from the principle of expediency the reasons why a Frenchman is bound in conscience to bear many things from his king, to which an Englishman is not obliged to submit. If the principles which I have endeavoured to establish are true, the answer to an enquiry into the different obligations of the members of different communities will flow from an equally obvious and less objectionable source. The inhabitants of the whole world are severally endowed with the same natural rights; and the difference in the degrees of authority to which the monarchs of neighbouring countries are entitled, is created by a difference in the laws to which their respective subjects give their consent.

7th: " The interest of the whole society " is binding upon every part of it." This rule, if confined to the internal regulations of the society, is perfectly consistent with the positions which I have maintained. I have repeatedly stated, that few of the duties which an individual owes to God are of higher concern than strenuous exertions for the welfare of those with whom he is united by the ties of social connection; and a similar conduct is in many cases required by strict justice. Yet however laudably his zeal may be exerted in enduring hardships, in submitting to losses, or in exposing himself to dangers for the sake of his fellow-subjects, it must be scrupulously restrained to those cases, in which it will not be attended with an unjust violation of the rights of other men.

As Mr. Paley professedly rests his most powerful objections to the doctrine, which ascribes the rights of government to the consent

sent of the subject, on the pernicious consequences with which he apprehends that doctrine necessarily to be burthened; and recommends his own principle of civil authority as peculiarly favourable to human happiness; I shall state the characteristic features of the two systems. The reader will judge whether the respective representations be fairly drawn; and will decide whether the principle of expediency or consent is the most favourable to the just authority of government, and to the peace and welfare of the people.

According to the positions which I have maintained, subjects have a right, not only to resist the legislature whenever it proceeds to an act of power unauthorised by the laws, but, further, to resume at any period the authority which they have delegated (unless they have entered into an express stipulation to the contrary) and to institute a new form of government, according to whatever plan they shall be inclined to adopt. These rights form a barrier against despotism, and afford ample scope for improvements in civil polity.

At

At the fame time confiderations are not wanting, by which the ftability of the fovereign power is fecured from the danger of unneceffary changes in the conftitution, and the community from the calamities of inteftine difcords and civil war. Every fubject is bound, as long as he continues a member of the ftate, to obey all fuch laws as the ftate has a right to enact, and determines to continue; and in eftimating the propriety of refifting the encroachments of the magiftrate, or of abetting any change in the conftitution, he is highly criminal in the fight of God, if a regard to the welfare of his fellow-fubjects be not one of the motives which have a principal influence on his mind.

But, though the profperity of his country muft be one of the leading objects of his care as a member of civil fociety, he is bound, as a being accountable to his Maker, to abftain from all attempts to promote it at the expenfe of juftice. He is to remember the facrednefs of the rights of others; and this confideration will preferve him from being mifled by miftaken patriotifm in his conduct towards foreigners; it will preferve him from

being

being deluded by miſtaken ideas of allegiance to concur in acts of tyranny towards his fellow-citizens.

On Mr. Paley's principles, the ſubject has a right, and is alſo bound in point of duty, to reſiſt the exiſting governors, whether uſurpers or not, and to join in affecting a change in the conſtitution, then, and then only, when ſuch ſteps will, in his opinion, conduce to the public welfare. According to this poſition, however tyrannical, unjuſt, or impious, the commands of government may be, if he[g] ſhould be ordered to deſtroy an innocent fellow-citizen; to ravage the territories of an ally; to embrace a religion which he knows to be idolatrous; in all theſe caſes, if he conceives that compliance will promote general expediency, compliance is his duty. Nay, he would act as meritorious a part in betraying his country, in ſetting fire to her dock-yards, or in blowing up her legiſlature, to promote

[g] The reader will recollect what I have quoted from Mr. Paley, in a former part of this treatiſe, that in his opinion caſes may ariſe in which every moral duty is ſuperſeded on the ground of general expediency.

the defigns of a foreign invader, if he fhould imagine that fuch a deed would, on the whole, be productive of advantage to mankind, as if, with contrary fentiments, he had hazarded his life in the breach for her defence. In like manner he is authorifed to violate every law, even though he fhould have perfonally engaged by promife or by oath on no plea whatever to difobey it; he is empowered, like Cade, to head a barbarous rebellion; like Felton, to murder the favourite of the monarch; like Damiens, to affaffinate the monarch himfelf; whenever his paffion or his fanaticifm induce him to believe that thefe outrages will in the end be fanctioned by utility. Nor is lefs latitude allowed by Mr. Paley to the difcretion of the governor than to that of the fubject. " The reafoning [h] which de-
" duces the authority of civil government
" from the will of God, and which collects
" that will from public expediency alone,
" binds us to the unreferved conclufion, that
" the jurifdiction of the magiftrate is limited
" by no confideration but that of general
" utility: in plainer terms, that, whatever

[h] Paley, Vol. II. Page 324.

" is

"is the subject to be regulated, it is lawful for him to interfere, *whenever* his interference, in its general tendency, appears (to the magistrate himself, as Mr. Paley afterwards says expressly)[1] to be conducive to the common interest." He is therefore authorised to violate at his discretion all the rights of his subjects, by whatever solemn engagements he may have bound himself to preserve them; he is obliged in conscience to trample on every law, human and divine, whenever such conduct accords with his notions of general expediency. If then he should be of opinion, that by assuming power in opposition to the will of the nation, and maintaining it by an army of mercenaries, he should promote the good of the people without impairing the happiness of mankind in general, he would be justified in his usurpation. If he should also think that lavishing the blood of his subjects in a crusade, and seizing half their property to defray the charge of the enterprise, would be an additional advantage to them, he would do no more than his duty in turning a deaf ear to their remon-

[1] Vol. II. Page 327.

strances,

strances, and in enforcing submission by the bayonet.—Nay, though he should not be able to satisfy himself that these proceedings would be for the interest of his people; yet, if he should fancy that GENERAL good would in some way be promoted by them; or if he should endeavour to promote it by putting his subjects into the hand of a neighbouring potentate as vassals; by selling them for slaves to a company of foreign merchants; or by introducing among them Popery or Paganism, and enforcing its reception by inquisitorial persecution; in each of these instances, according to Mr. Paley's principle, he would merit the gratitude of mankind, and the approbation of his God.

THE END.

www.ingramcontent.com/pod-product-compliance
Lightning Source LLC
Chambersburg PA
CBHW020842160426
43192CB00007B/755